Wallace Bruce

The Hudson River by daylight

New York to Albany

Wallace Bruce

The Hudson River by daylight
New York to Albany

ISBN/EAN: 9783337377434

Printed in Europe, USA, Canada, Australia, Japan

Cover: Foto ©Andreas Hilbeck / pixelio.de

More available books at **www.hansebooks.com**

THE
HUDSON RIVER
BY
DAYLIGHT.

NEW YORK TO ALBANY,

SARATOGA SPRINGS, LAKE GEORGE, LAKE CHAMPLAIN, PLATTSBURG, THE ADIRONDACKS, MONTREAL, THE THOUSAND ISLANDS, NIAGARA FALLS, WATKINS' GLEN, RICHFIELD SPRINGS, COOPERSTOWN, SHARON, HOWE'S CAVE, THE GREEN MOUNTAINS, MANCHESTER, MIDDLETOWN AND LEBANON SPRINGS.

THE FIRST DESCRIPTIVE ANALYSIS OF THE HUDSON EVER PUBLISHED.

Entered according to Act of Congress, in the year 1873, by
WALLACE BRUCE,
in the Office of the Librarian of Congress at Washington.

PUBLISHED BY
JOHN FEATHERSTON,
Proprietor of News Stands on the Day Line of Steamboats.
NEW YORK, 1873.

HUDSON RIVER GUIDE-BOARD

FROM

NEW YORK TO ALBANY.

What a Person wishes to See and Know About the Hudson.

A Condensed Sketch of the Prominent Points of Interest, presenting at once an Index to Book, Map, and River.

As the boat leaves the pier an extended view is obtained of the upper bay of New York—miles of shipping; and, in the southern distance, twelve miles of Staten Island.

Trinity, St. Paul's, and St. John's. The three pointed church spires, Trinity to the south, and St. John's to the North.

Prominent Buildings. Equitable and New York Life Insurance Companys, near Trinity spire, and the New Bennett Building, on Nassau street, corner Fulton.

Jersey City, on the opposite shore, also lined with the docks of ocean steamers, once known as Paulus Hook.

Hoboken, on west side, a short distance above Jersey City.

Castle Hill, a rocky promontory above Hoboken, crowned with the mansion of the Stevens family.

Elysian Fields, above Castle Hill, sloping to the river.

Bergen Heights rise in the background, west of Hoboken.

Manhattan Market, a fine brick building on the New York side, at the intersection of Tenth Avenue and Thirty-Fourth Street.

Weehawken, the scene of the duel between Hamilton and Burr, on the west bank, above the Elysian Fields.

Sixty-Fifth Street, marked by a rocky bluff on the New York side.

Mystery. The seven-story white building on the west, above Weehawken, is *only* a lager-beer brewery.

Jones Hill, on New York side. The long wooden building, near the river, is a shooting-gallery.

Lunatic Asylum, known as Bloomingdale Hospital, on the New York side, between 115th and 120th streets.

Manhattanville, a city suburb in the neighborhood of 132d street.

Carmansville (the home of Audubon, the great ornithologist), a city suburb at 152d street, where you see a red building (sugar refinery).

River House. Hotel near the river, on the New York side, once called the Claremont Hotel.

Trinity Cemetery, above the hotel.

New York Institute for Deaf and Dumb. A large building of yellow Milwaukee brick, a little above Carmansville. Will accommodate 450 persons. Incorporated 1817.

Tillie Teudlem, on west side, opposite Carmansville. Hotel, dock, &c.

Fort Lee, about a mile above Tillie Teudlem. The site of the old fort is marked by a white fence on the bluff.

Palisades commence at Fort Lee, and extend fifteen miles. A sheer wall of trap-rock, from 250 to 550 feet high, covered with trees that seem in the distance like a fringe of shrubbery.

Washington Heights, on New York side, between 181st and 185th streets. Almost opposite Fort Lee.

Fort Washington. The site of the old fort was near the residence of the late James Gordon Bennett. The residence will be distinguished among the trees by its gilded dome.

Jeffrey's Hook. A point jutting into the river below Washington Heights.

Innwood. A little station on the Hudson River Railroad, above the heights. This place was once known as Tubbie Hook.

Palisade Mountain House. Large hotel on the Palisades, opposite Innwood.

Spuyten Duyvel Creek (Harlem River), on the east, or New York side, meets the Hudson. It reaches, in a southeasterly direction, to the East River, forming the island of Manhattan, or New York. The island is twelve miles long, averaging about two miles in width,—wedge-shape, pointing to the Battery.

Spuyten Duyvel. A cluster of houses above the creek.

Westchester Heights rise above the village of Spuyten Duyvel.

Riverdale Station. First station on the Hudson River Railroad above Spuyten Duyvel.

The Convent and Academy of Mount St. Vincent. Fifteen miles from New York. The castle-like building in front, once known as Fonthill, built by Edwin Forrest.

Yonkers. A fine, thriving town, seventeen miles from New York. Near the landing we see the neat depot of the Hudson River Railroad. Also, the principal news depot between New York and Albany. John Featherston, proprietor.

C. H. Lilienthal's Residence. A brown building, with square tower, two miles above the landing.

Spring-Hill Grove. Also on the east bank, and near by the ruins of a *pickle* and *preserve* factory.

Dudley's Grove. Just beyond.

Indian Head. The highest point of the Palisades, about opposite the Grove.

Hastings-on-the-Hudson. Four miles north of Yonkers, on the east side. The sugar-refinery near the bank is the largest on the river.

Dobbs' Ferry. On the east side, above Hastings, twenty-two miles from New York. The river now widens into Tappan Bay.

Piermont, with its long pier, on the west side, almost opposite. This was once the terminus of the Erie Railroad, and marks the boundary-line between New York and New Jersey.

Nevis. Once the home of Col. James Hamilton, on the east side, above Dobbs' Ferry; long columns in front of house.

Cottinet Place. Built of Caen Stone, near Nevis; pronounced the most elegant residence on the Hudson.

Cyrus W. Field's Residence. Also between Dobbs' Ferry and Irvington.

Irvington. Four miles north of Dobbs' Ferry, on east side; once known as Dearman's. Name changed in honor of Washington Irving.

Sunnyside. Half a mile above Irvington Station; once called Wolfert's Roost; near the river, and hardly visible through the trees.

Cunningham Castle. Stone mansion, with pointed tower, on the hill.

Paulding Manor. The white marble edifice, of Elizabethan architecture. The hot-house, with cupola, cost of itself $100,000.

Bierstadt, the artist, brown stone house, with cupola, south of the Paulding manor. Mr. Halsted's residence (of the old firm of Halsted, Haines, & Co.), in immediate neighborhood.

Tarrytown. On east side, three miles above Irvington; twenty-six miles from New York.

Sleepy Hollow. A little north of Tarrytown. The old Dutch church is visible with a glass, and the quiet graveyard where Irving is buried.

Ex-Mayor Kingsland's. Two summer-houses, or stationary bird-cages, will be noticed on the east bank, just above Tarrytown. Here is the home of Mr Kingsland.

William Aspinwall's Residence. Above Tarrytown; brown square tower; the largest on the river.

Johnny Dean's, and "his own Mary Ann." Near the river, below Mr. Aspinwall's, and a little to the north, is the place where Johnny Dean met "his own Mary Ann."

Nyack. Opposite Tarrytown. (In the channel the ferryboat connects with the Day Line.) The large building a little south of the village is the Rockland Female Seminary.

Ramapo Mountains. Above Nyack, on the west side; known by navigators as the Hook, or Point-no-Point. They lie in little headlands, 500 or 600 feet high, and reach most of the way from Nyack to Haverstraw. (The point is, in fact, an illusion; was once called Verdrietege's Hook; now sometimes styled Rockland Lake Point.)

Sing Sing. On east side, six miles above Tarrytown. The white buildings near the river-bank, south of the village, are the State Prison.

Rockland Lake. Almost opposite, on the west bank, between two hills. This is the source of the Hackensack river, and the great ice-quarry for New York.

Croton River, on the east bank, meets the Hudson about one mile above Sing Sing, where you see the drawbridge of the Hudson River Railroad.

Croton Point. Just above Croton River.

Teller's Point. That part of Croton Point which juts into the Hudson. Here is Underhill's grapery, and this point separates Tappan Zee from Haverstraw Bay.

Croton. Just above the Point, on the eastern side.

Haverstraw Bay. The widest part of the Hudson—five miles from Haverstraw to Croton. Held as it were in the arms of Croton Point on the south, and Verplank's Point on the north.

Haverstraw. On west bank. Two miles of brick-yard, north of Haverstraw, line the river

High-thorn, or Thornhill. The highest peak near the village, to the southwest.

Treason Hill. North of Haverstraw, where Arnold and Andre met, at the house of Joshua Hett Smith.

Grassy Point. On west side, two miles above Haverstraw.

Montrasses Point. On the east side.

Minnissickongo Creek flows into the Hudson, just above Grassy Point

Stony Point. One mile above Grassy Point, on west side. The house and lighthouse built on the site of the old fort, and in part of the same material.

Verplank's Point. On east side, directly opposite. The river here is only half a mile wide. This was known as King's Ferry, at and before the Revolution. The Point is now *adorned* with brick-yards.

Tompkins Cove. Lime-kiln and quarry on west side.

Peekskill. On east bank, above Verplank's Point, forty-two miles from New York.

Kidd's Point. Now called Caldwell's Landing, on west side. The steamer turns this point almost at right angles, and enters the Highlands.

Dunderberg, or Dunderbarrack, a mountain on west bank, about 1,000 feet high.

Iona Island. Grapery, and fine pic-nic grounds.

The Nameless Highland. On east side. It rises in two peaks, something like Dumbarton Crag, on the river Clyde.

The Race. The river channel is so termed by navigators, between Iona Island and the east bank.

Anthony's Nose. Prominent feature of the river, 1500 feet high. The railroad tunnel is near the river. In front of tunnel a hole in the rock. Here was fastened one end of the chain that was thrown across the channel to obstruct British ships during the Revolution.

Montgomery Creek, on west side, empties into the Hudson about opposite the point of Anthony's Nose.

Fort Clinton was on the south side of this Creek, and *Fort Montgomery* on the north side.

Highland Lake, about one mile in circumference, on the south side of Montgomery Creek. The site is marked by an ice-house.

Sugar-Loaf. Turning Anthony's Nose we get a good view of Sugar-Loaf Mountain to the north. Cone-shaped, like Ailsa Crag, between Belfast and Glasgow.

David McGuire's Residence, south of Sugar-Loaf, on east side.

Beverly Dock, on east bank, where Arnold fled to the "Vulture." A little boat-house now marks the point.

Hamilton Fish has a residence on the bluff under Sugar-Loaf. A brick house, with flat roof.

"Benny Havens, Oh!" As the steamer approaches Cozzen's Landing we see a small two-story house, with verandah. Here still lives Benny Havens, the original of the West Point and College song.

Parry House, south of Cozzen's Hotel, near the river. Picturesque ruins of an old mill in front.

Buttermilk Falls. A cascade above the Parry House.

Cozzen's Hotel. On a rock two hundred feet above the river. Highland Falls Village lies behind the bluff, a place of about 3,000 inhabitants. (Not seen from the river.)

Cozzen's Landing. A romantic road cut through the rock leads from the landing to the hotel.

West-Point Landing. A short mile above Cozzen's Landing. Academy, Government Buildings, Parade Grounds, &c., on the finest elevation on the Hudson.

Garrison. Opposite West Point, on east bank.

The Highland House. On east side, about half a mile from the river, on a magnificent plateau, inclosed by the North and South Redoubt Mountains. Indian Falls in the vicinity.

Kosciusco's Monument. Seen on the west side, above West-Point Landing.

Fort Putnam, 596 feet high, overlooks the river, on the west side. A gray and veteran ruin of '76.

West-Point Lighthouse. The Hudson here turns a right angle. Roe's Hotel has a fine look off to the north. West-Point Village around the Point.

Constitution Island, opposite the Point. Here are also seen ruins of '76. Near the river, home of Miss Warner, author of "Queechy" and "The Wide,

ROAD TO COZZENS' DOCK.

"The main road, partly cut like a sloping terrace in the rocks, is picturesque at every turn, but especially near the landing, where pleasant glimpses of the river and its water craft may be seen."—*From Lossing's "Hudson, From the Wilderness to the Sea."*

Wide World,"—a neat white cottage, surrounded by trees, above the boat-house. A chain was also thrown across from this Island to West Point.

The Two Brothers. Twin rocks above Constitution Island, covered in high water.

Old Cro'-Nest Mountain. On west side, above the Point, 1,418 feet high. Scene of Rodman Drake's "Culprit Fay."

Kidd's Plug Cliff. The precipice fronting the river, toward the northern peak of Cro'-Nest.

Cold Spring. On east bank, opposite Old Cro'-Nest.

Undercliff. A short distance north of Cold Spring, once the home of Geo. P. Morris, on an elevated plateau above the river.

Mount Taurus, or Bull Hill, above Undercliff.

Little Stony Point. Under Mount Taurus. Named from resemblance to Stony Point, south of the Highlands.

Break Neck. Above Mount Taurus, on the east side. Here was once the Turk's Face, now blasted away. It is said a man did it in spite, and was soon after "blown up" himself.

Storm King. On west bank, above Old Cro'-Nest. It was once known as Butter Hill, and years ago as Klinkersberg. Its present name was given by Willis. This is the highest point of the Highlands—about 1800 feet.

Beacon Hill is now seen on the east bank, after passing Break-Neck—about 1471 feet high.

Fishkill Mountains trend off to the northeast, across the southern part of Duchess County.

Cornwall, with its pleasant Summer Homes on west side above Storm King.

Pollipel's Island. At upper portal of the Highlands, near the east bank.

Idlewild. Once home of N. P. Willis, on west side, about one mile above Cornwall. (Gothic house north of an open field, the 3rd above a high towered building.)

New Windsor, on west, side about 4 miles north of Cornwall, once the rival of Newburgh: now a brick-yard.

Newburgh Bay. The river here widens into one of the finest bays on the Hudson.

Washington's Head Quarters. As the boat approaches the city, we see the Head Quarters of Washington; a flag-staff marks the point. The old building is also seen with tall chimneys and steep roof almost sloping to the foundations.

Newburgh City. Rising in natural terraces.

Fishkill Landing. On east side opposite Newburgh.

Low Point, or *Carthage.* On east side above Fishkill.

Devil's Dans Kammer. Flat rock on the west side, covered with Cedars, named the Devil's Dancing Chamber by Hendrick Hudson from an Indian Pow-wow witnessed here.

New Hamburgh, above Low Point, on the east side at the mouth of Wappinger's Creek.

Hampton Point, opposite New Hamburgh. Here are the finest white cedars on the river.

Marlborough. Also on west side above Hampton Point.

Barnegat, on east side.

Shawangunk Mountains, on the west side reach away in the distance toward the Catskills.

Milton. The raspberry and strawberry town on west side above Marlborough.

Locust Grove. Large brown house on east side, with square tower, home of the late Prof. S. F. B. Morse.

Poughkeepsie Cemetery, on east side; old Livingston Place directly above on a wooded point; near by a large rolling mill is being built.

Poughkeepsie, 74 miles from New York. Queen City of the Hudson. Situated for the most part on a plateau about 200 feet above the river.

Riverview Military Academy. Large brick building on a fine eminence.

Buckeye Mower Manufactory, Adriance, Platt & Co., proprietors. Fine buildings, near the river bank.

Kaal Rock, near Poughkeepsie landing. Its name signifies Barren Rock.

Vassar Brewery. Long white buildings above the landing.

New Paltz Landing, opposite Poughkeepsie. The west banks here are also fine and picturesque.

Poughkeepsie Water Works. On east bank about one mile above the landing. The water is forced from the river to a reservoir on Academy Hill. The hill is crowned by Hon. George Morgan's residence, built after the model of the Parthenon.

Mr. Winslow's Residence, on east bank.

The Insane Asylum. About two miles above Poughkeepsie.

Joseph Boorman, First President of the Hudson River R. R., lives about 3 miles north of Insane Asylum, where an iron bridge crosses the track. A pretty stone summer house on the point.

Hyde Park, on east side, six miles north of Poughkeepsie. Connected with Poughkeepsie by a succession of villas; the finest drive in the country.

Placentia, on west side, about one mile above Hyde Park. Once home of James K. Paulding, friend of Washington Irving.

Doctor Hussack's Estate, on east side. The front painted blue and white. Corinthian pillars.

Esopus Island and Meadows, on west side.

Staatsburgh, above Hyde Park on east side. Mr. Pell's great apple orchard almost opposite; stone store-house near the river. The river begins to widen into Rondout Bay.

Rhinecliff, or *Rhinebeck Landing,* on the east side.

Rondout, or *City of Kingston,* on west side. A little south of Rondout is Port Ewen, known as the "Deserted Village."

Rokeby. Wm. B. Astor's residence, above Rhinecliff, with tower and pointed roof.

Barrytown, on east side.

Cruger's Island. 2 miles above Barrytown, with an imported ruin from Italy on the south end of Island.

Tivoli, on east side, 100 miles from New York.

Glasgo. A little south of Tivoli, on west side.

Saugerties. A little to the north of Tivoli, on west side, at the mouth of Esopus Creek.

Malden. Above Saugerties, on west side. Dock covered with blue stone

Clermont. Above Tivoli, on east side. The original Livingston manor.

West Camp. On west side, above Malden.

Four County Island. Near west bank; the "meeting point" of Duchess, Columbia, Greene, and Ulster.

Germantown. On east side. 105 miles from New York.

Man in the Mountain. From this point we get a fine view of the reclining giant. You can trace it by the following outline:—the peak to the south is the *knee;* the next to the north the *breast;* and two or three above this, the *chin,* the *nose,* and the *forehead.*

(VIEW ON THE HUDSON.)
Soldiers Memorial Fountain, Poughkeepsie.

Round Top. The highest point of the Catskills. 4000 feet high.

Catskill Mountain House, will be seen in a clear day like a snow drift. left on the mountains.

Livingston. On east side. A small station on the Hudson River Rail Road, about 4 miles above Germantown.

Catskill. On west side, just above Catskill Creek.

Prospect Point Hotel. On a fine eminence to north of landing.

Church, the Artist, has a new residence on east side on a hill, almost opposite Catskill.

Mount Merino. On east side, about two miles up the river. Owned by Col. O. D. Ashley.

Hudson. On east side. Promenade hill just above the landing.

Athens. Opposite. Hudson River Depot for freight. large building near the river.

Stockport. On east side, four miles north of Hudson, near the mouth of Columbiaville Creek. This creek is formed by the union of the Kinderhook and Claverack Creeks.

Four-mile-Point. On west side, about 125 feet high; four miles from Hudson and four from Coxsackie. Narrow channel for 2 miles close to the west shore. Average about 850 feet wide. At upper end of narrow channel Grape vine dock and a Grapery of 100 acres.

Coxsackie. On west side, 8 miles from Hudson.

Newton Hook; opposite Coxsackie; the wooded point is called Prospect Grove.

Stuyvesant. On the east side. Once called Kinderhook Landing.

Schodack Island. On east side, about two miles above Stuyvesant. The island is about 3 miles long, covered mostly with broom corn.

New Baltimore. About opposite the centre of Schodack Island; fifteen miles from Hudson and fifteen from Albany. The government dykes begin opposite New Baltimore.

Barren Island. Site of the famous "Castle of Rensselaerstien." (vid. Irving's Knickerbocker). Four counties also meet here,—Columbia, Rensselaer, Greene, and Albany. Island ½ mile long, ¼ mile wide.

Coeymans. Right above Barren Island; connected with a dyke. Above Coeymans is what is known as the Coeymans' Cross Over.

Shad Island. The first island to the westward above Coeymans; 3 miles long; old Indian fishing ground.

Nine-mile-Tree. On east bank. *Castleton.* One mile above Tree, on east side. *Campbell's Island.* On lower end a light.
Cedar Hill Dock. Opposite this light.
Staats Island. Above Campbell's Island. This was settled by the Staats family before the arrival of the Van Rensselaers', and never belonged to the Patroon. The house is about 200 years old; at least a part of it, and mostly built of stone.

The Overslaugh reaches from Van Wies' Point; (the first point above Cedar Hill,) about two miles up the river.

Albany is now near at hand, and we see to the south the Convent of the Sacred Heart; to the north the Cathedral, the Capitol, the State House the City Hall, &c. *Greenbush* opposite. Connected with Albany by ferries and two fine substantial bridges.

Troy, on east bank, six miles from Albany. *West Troy*, opposite.

Thus, in brief, we have traced the river, as it were step by step, from New York to the head of tide-water; and we have endeavored to make these pages a practical *Guide-Board* to the various points of historic and legendary interest which literally fill our river valley. The Hand, whose index finger has thus far pointed north, *opens* at Albany, and with five fingers points to—.

1. Cooperstown, Sharon and Richfield Springs.
2. Niagara Falls and Watkins Glen.
3. Saratoga, Lake George and Plattsburg.
4. Montreal, and the Thousand Islands.
5. The White and Green Mountains.

To each of these summer routes we will call your attention, at the close of the Hudson sketch.

And now, as we present our Hudson Handbook for the fifth year to the traveling public, we wish to express our acknowledgments to the gentlemanly captains and pilots of the day-boats, for many facts here presented in this analysis,—*facts* which we could not have gathered either from books or libraries. We would also acknowledge the kindness of our friend Mr. Benson J. Lossing, and his publishers, Messrs. Virtue & Yorston, 12 Dey Street, in allowing us a selection of their beautiful cuts,which have made the "Hudson, from the Wilderness to the Sea," a book without a rival, either in England or America. W. B.

THE TRAVELERS INSURANCE CO.
OF HARTFORD, CONN.

Cash Assets, - - - - - $2,350,000.

Grants Everything Desirable in

LIFE OR ACCIDENT INSURANCE.

The Travelers Insurance Company offers peculiar inducements to persons desiring Life Insurance, in its low rates of premium, its liberal and definite contract, its sensible all-cash plan, its freedom from complication and mystery, its cash assets of $150 to every $100 of liability, and its economy and careful management.

The Travelers Insurance Company calls the attention of business men, professional men, and men of all trades and occupations (between the ages of 18 and 65), to the fact that it is the only company in America writing yearly or monthly policies of insurance against general accidents — that such policies grant a fixed sum ($1,000 to $10,000) in case of death by accident, or a weekly indemnity ($5 to $50) for loss of time caused by non-fatal accident — that the cost of such a policy is but $5 to $10 a year for each $1,000 insured, for men not engaged in hazardous occupations.

☞ *For insurance, apply to any Agent, or write to the Company. Accident policies written without delay. Information as to rates, classification, etc., furnished freely on application.*

THE HUDSON.

The Hudson has been called the Shate-muck, the Mohegan, the Manhattan, the Noordt Montaigne, the Mauritius, the North River, and the River of the Mountains. It was called the Hudson River, not by the Dutch as generally stated, but by the English, as Henry Hudson was an Englishman, although he sailed from a Dutch port, with a Dutch crew, and a Dutch vessel. The river was called the Mauritius in a letter to

OLOFFE VAN KORTLANDT'S DREAM.

the "High and mighty Lords" of Holland, written November 5, 1626. It was called the North River to distinguish it from the Delaware, called the South River. The Spaniards called it the River of the Mountains. It was discovered in the year 1609. The town of Communipaw was founded soon after, and according to Knickerbocker,—whose quiet humor is always read and re-read with pleasure,—might justly be considered the mother colony of our glorious city: for lo! the sage Oloffe Van

Kortlandt dreamed a dream, and the good St. Nicholas came riding over the tops of the trees, and descended upon the island of Manhattan and sat himself down and smoked, "and the smoke ascended into the sky, and formed a cloud overhead; and Oloffe bethought him, and he hastened and climbed up to the top of one of the tallest trees, and saw that the smoke spread over a great extent of country; and, as he considered it more attentively, he fancied that the great volume assumed a variety of marvelous forms, where, in dim obscurity, he saw shadowed out palaces and domes and lofty spires, all of which lasted but a moment, and then passed away." So New York, like Alba Longa and Rome, and other cities of antiquity, was under the immediate care of its tutelar saint. Its destiny was foreshadowed, for now the palaces and domes and lofty spires are real and genuine, and something more than dreams are made of.

NEW YORK, by virtue of its admirable position, soon became the headquarters of the fur trade. The merchants of North Holland organized a company, and obtained from the States General, in 1614, a charter to trade in the New Netherlands; and, soon after, a colony built a few houses and a fort near the Battery. The entire island was purchased from the Indians, 1624, for the sum of sixty guilders, or about twenty-four dollars. A fort was also built at Albany in 1623, and known as Fort Aurania, or Fort Orange. New York was called for years New Amsterdam; but in the year 1664, when these forts were surrendered to the English, the two settlements took the names of New York and Albany, in honor of the Duke of York and Albany. In June, 1636, the first land was bought on Long Island; and in 1667 the Ferry Town, opposite New York, was known by the name Breuckelen, signifying broken land, but the name was not generally accepted until after the Revolution. Bergen was the oldest settlement in New Jersey. It was founded in 1616 by the Dutch colonists to the New Netherlands, and received its name from Bergen, in Norway. Paulus Hook, or Jersey City, in 1638 was the farm of William Kieft, Director-General of the Dutch West India Company.

So much for the early history of New York and the surrounding cities, which have sprung up as it were in a day; for, as late as 1800 the city of Brooklyn had only 2,000 inhabitants, and, in 1820, Jersey City only 300.

HENDRICH HUDSON AND THE HALF MOON.—The first voyagers up the Hudson were, as before stated, Hendrich Hudson and his crew of the "Half Moon." He anchored off Sandy Hook September 3d, 1609, and remained off the Hook a little more than a week. He then passed through the Narrows, and anchored in what is now called Newark Bay; on the 12th resumed his voyage, and, drifting with the tide, anchored over night on the 13th just above Yonkers; on the 14th passed Tappan and Haverstraw Bays, entered the Highlands, and anchored for the night near West Point. On the morning of the 15th entered Newburgh Bay, and reached Catskill on the 16th, Athens on the 17th, and Castleton and Albany on the 18th, and then sent out an exploring boat as far as Waterford. His return voyage began on the 23d. He anchored again in Newburgh Bay the 25th, and reached Stony Point October 1st; reached Sandy Hook the 4th, and then returned to Europe. The "Half Moon" was becalmed off Sandy Hook, and the people of the mountains came to see them. We might also add, in this place, that it is claimed by some that Hendrich Hudson was the first to call the river "The River of the Mountains," a name which the Spaniards and French afterward adopted. The Iroquois called it the Co-hat-a-tea. The Mohegans and Lenapes called it the Mohegan, or Mah-i-can-i-tuk—"the continually flowing waters,"—probably from the tide, which rises and falls from New York to Troy. The name Mauritius was given in honor of Prince Maurice, of Nassau, in the year 1611.

THE OLD REACHES.—The Hudson was divided at one time by the old navigators, long before the days of "propelling steam," into fourteen Reaches—one of which names is still used in the poetic name of Claverack, the Clover-Reach. We will give some of these as a matter of historic interest:—

The *Great Chip-Rock* Reach—the Palisades—were known by the old Dutch settlers as the "Great Chip," and so styled in the Bergen Deed of Purchase, viz., the great chip above Weehawken.

The *Tappan* Reach, on the east side of which dwelt the Manhattans, on the west side the Saulrickans and the Tappans. The third reach extends upward to a narrow point called *Haverstroo;* then comes the *Seylmaker's* reach, and then *Crescent* reach; next *Hoge's* reach, and then *Vorsen* reach, which extends to Klinkersberg, or Storm King, the northern portal of the Highlands. This is succeeded by *Fisher's* reach, where, on the east side, once dwelt a race of savages called Pachami. "This reach," in the language of De Laet, "extends to another narrow pass, where, on the west, is a point of land which juts out, covered with sand, opposite a bend in the river, on which another nation of savages —the Waoranecks—have their abode at a place called Esopus. Next, another reach, called *Claverack;* then *Backerack;* next the *Playsier* reach, and *Vaste* reach, as far as Hinnenhock; then the *Hunters'* reach, as far as Kinderhook; and Fisher's Hook, near Shad Island, over which, on the east side, dwell the Mohegans." These old reaches and names have long passed away from the use or memory of even the river pilots, and may, perhaps, possess interest only to the antiquarian. But there are

FIVE DIVISIONS, OR REACHES, OF THE HUDSON,

which we imagine will have interest for all, as they present in brief an analysis easy to be remembered—divisions marked by something more substantial than sentiment or fancy, expressing five distinct characteristics—

GRANDEUR, REPOSE, SUBLIMITY, THE PICTURESQUE, BEAUTY.

1. THE PALISADES, an unbroken wall of rock for fifteen miles— GRANDEUR.
2. THE TAPPAN ZEE, surrounded by the sloping hills of Nyack, Tarrytown, and Sleepy Hollow—REPOSE.
3. THE HIGHLANDS, where the Hudson for twenty miles plays "hide and seek" with "hills rock-ribbed and ancient as the sun,"—SUBLIMITY.
4. THE HILLSIDES for miles above and below Poughkeepsie—THE PICTURESQUE.
5. THE CATSKILLS, on the west, throned in queenly dignity—BEAUTY.

THE PALISADES—GRANDEUR.

"And as you nearer draw, each wooded height
Puts off the azure hues by distance given,
And slowly break upon the enamored sight
Ravine, crag, field, and wood, in colors true and bright."

We know of no other river in the world which presents so great a variety of views as the Hudson. Throughout its whole extent, from the "Wilderness to the Sea," from the Adirondacks to Staten Island, there is a combination of the finest pictures; and each division which we have indicated seems to illustrate some of the best scenery of the old world. With only a slight stretch of fancy, we imagine the tourist may find Loch Katrine "nestled" among the mountains of our own Highlands; will see in the Catskills the Sunset Mountains of Arran; and in the Palisades the Giant's Causeway of Ireland.

In reference to this idea of picture combination, we can appropriately cite the words of George William Curtis, who pronounces the Hudson grander than the Rhine. He says, "The Danube has in part glimpses of such grandeur. The Elbe has sometimes such delicately pencilled effects. But no European river is so lordly in its bearing, none flows in such state to the sea." Thackeray, also, in his "Virginians," has given to the Hudson the verdict of beauty; and we imagine this is the unprejudiced opinion of tourists and travelers.

The Palisades, or Great Chip Rock, as they were known by the old Dutch settlers, present the same bold front to the river that the Giants' Causeway does to the ocean. We should judge these rocks to be of about the same height and the same extent. The Palisades are from two hundred and fifty to six hundred feet high, and extend about fifteen miles, from Fort Lee to the hills of Rockland County. As the basaltic trap-rock is one of the oldest geological formations, we might still appropriately style the Palisades "a *chip* of the old block." They separate the valley of the Hudson from the valley of the Hackensack. The Hackensack rises in Rockland Lake, within two or three hundred yards of the Hudson, and the rivers flow thirty miles side by side, but are effectually separated from each other by a wall more substantial than even the 2,000 mile structure of the "Heathen Chinee."

WEEHAWKEN, one of the sad historic spots of the Hudson, was much frequented years ago; but the place is hardly ever visited in these latter days. In fact, everything is changed. The narrow ledge of rock where Hamilton fell in a duel with Aaron Burr on the morning of July 11, 1804, has made way for the West Side Railroad; and we are not sorry that the last vestige connected with a "false code of honor" has been removed.

DUELLING GROUND, WEEHAWKEN.
(From Lossing's "Hudson, from the Wilderness to the Sea.")

The St. Andrew's Society, a short time after the duel, erected a monument on the spot to the memory of the great statesman, but that too was gradually destroyed by visitors, and taken away in pieces, souvenirs of a sad tragedy.

SPUYTEN DUYVEL CREEK.—This is the first point of special legendary interest, and takes its name from a highly chivalric and poetic incident. It seems that the famous Antony Van Corlear was despatched one evening with an important message up the Hudson. When he arrived at this creek, the wind was high, the elements were in an uproar, and no boatman at hand. "For a short time," it is said, "he vapored like an impatient ghost upon the brink, and then, bethinking himself of the urgency of his errand, took a hearty embrace of his stone bottle, swore most valorously that he would swim across *en spijt en Duyvel* (in spite of the Devil) and daringly plunged into the stream. Luckless Antony! Scarce had he buffeted half way over when he was observed to struggle violently, as if battling with the spirit of the waters. Instinctively he put his trumpet to his mouth, and giving a vehement blast—sank forever to the bottom."

Passing the Convent and Academy of Mount St. Vincent, a fine structure on the east bank of the river, we come to

YONKERS, where Hendrich Hudson anchored one September evening, 1609. In the quaint language of those days, he "found a loving people, who attained great age." It is also generally believed that this was the place where Hendrich Hudson and his mate, Robert Juet, made that sage experiment, gravely recorded in the narrative of the discovery. "Our master and his mate determined to try some of the chief men of the country, whether they had any treachery in them; so they took them down into the cabin, and gave them so much wine and aqua vitæ that they were all very merric. In the end one of them was drunk, and that was strange to them, for they could not tell how to take it." One thing is certain, they learned how, as soon as they had opportunity—the only branch of civilization for which they appear to have had a natural taste. It is moreover said that the effect of this imported jugglery was decidedly strange, and soon after Hendrich's departure it came to be believed by the red men, who had seen the *zigzag* effect of fire-water on their brethren, that the Hudson must, at some period of the world's history, have become *inebriated,* to have made such a winding channel to the sea, and they instituted a search for the fire-water fountain. Of course they were unable to find the mysterious fountain; but the real legend is one of the oldest and therefore most *reliable* of our river traditions. This is the mouth of the Neperan, or Sawmill River, and here, in an obscure nook of the Hudson, west of the creek, is a large rock, which was called Mecch-keek-assin, or Amackasin, the great stone to which the Indians paid reverence as an evidence of the permanency and immutability of their deity.

It is generally said that Yonkers derived its name from Yonk-herr—the young heir, or young sir, of the Phillipsie manor. The English and Scotch word, however, as used by Shakespeare and Burns (viz., *yonker* and *younkers*) makes a voyage to a foreign language quite unnecessary.

The old manor house, near the river and above the landing, was purchased a short time ago by the village of Yonkers, and converted for the most part into offices for transacting town affairs. The older portion of the house was built in 1682; the present front in 1745. The woodwork is very interesting, and the ceilings, the large hall, and wide fireplace. In the room pointed out as Washington's room, the fireplace still retains the old tiles, "illustrating familiar passages in Bible history," fifty on each side, looking as clear as if they were made but yesterday. The town is growing very rapidly, and is almost a part of the great metropolis.

HASTINGS, four miles north of Yonkers and twenty-one from New York, is almost opposite the highest point of the Palisades, viz., "Indian Head." Here, it is said, Garibaldi used to spend his Sundays with Italian friends, at the time that he was "keeping a soap and candle factory on Staten Island."

DOBBS' FERRY is the next village above Hastings, on the east side, named after an old Swedish ferryman. It is the scene of a romantic story, long ago put in verse, and styled the "Legend of Dobbs' Ferry, or the Marital Fate of Hendrich and Katrina." The river now widens into a beautiful bay, known as the Mediterranean Sea of the New Netherlands, and we come to our second division.

TAPPAN ZEE—REPOSE.

"Cool shades and dews are round my way,
And silence of the early day,
'Mid the dark rocks that watch his bed
Glitters the mighty Hudson spread
Unrippled, save by drops that fall
From shrubs that fringe his mountain wall;
And o'er the clear still water swells
The music of the Sabbath bells."

The Palisades now lose their wall-like character, and break away in little headlands to the north and northwest; and now, as we pass PIERMONT, on the west side, we leave behind us the New Jersey wall, which was almost enough to "keep her out of the Union," and are entirely within the jurisdiction of the Empire State—the New Jersey line is only a short distance below Piermont. The pier of the Erie railroad, which here juts into the river, is about one mile in length, and gives the name to the village. The boulevard from this point to Rockland Lake, passing through Nyack, will soon be one of the finest drives on the Hudson. About two miles from Piermont is the old village of Tappan, where Andre was executed.

IRVINGTON is about opposite Piermont, twenty-four miles from New York. The river is here about three miles wide, and the sloping hills that look over this tranquil bay are literally covered with beautiful villas and charming grounds. About half a mile above the depot and near the river bank, almost hid in foliage, is

SUNNYSIDE, the great classic and poetic spot of our country—the home of Washington Irving, who laid the corner-stone of American literature. Fifty years ago the English critic sneeringly asked, "Who reads an American book?" Irving quietly answered the question, and carried the war into the enemy's country by writing "Bracebridge Hall," "Westminster Abbey," and "Stratford-on-Avon;" and his name is cherished to-day in England almost as fondly as in our own country. A few years ago it was our good fortune to pass a few days in the very centre of "Merrie England," in that quiet town on the Avon, and we found the name of Irving almost as reverently regarded as that of the immortal Shakespeare. The sitting-room in the "**Red Horse Hotel**," where he was disturbed in his midnight reverie, is still called Irving's room, and the walls hung with portraits taken at different periods of his life. Mine host said that visitors from every land were as much interested in this room as in Shakespeare's birthplace. The remark may have been intensified to flatter an American visitor, but there are few names dearer to the Anglo-Saxon race than that on the plain headstone in the burial-yard of Sleepy Hollow.

In Irving's essay of "Wolfert's Roost" (the old name of Sunnyside) he describes his home very aptly as "made up of gable-ends, and full of angles and corners as an old cocked hat. It is said, in fact, to have been modelled after the cocked hat of Peter the Headstrong, as the Escurial of Spain was modelled after the gridiron of the blessed St. Laurence." The late Napoleon III. was at one time a visitor at Sunnyside; and here, in 1842, Daniel Webster paid Irving a visit, with appointment and credentials as Minister to Spain.

TARRYTOWN is also on the east side, about three miles north of Irvington. Its name was derived from the old Dutch word Tarwe-town, or wheat-town, although Knickerbocker's natural philosophy imagined that it arose from the tarrying of husband at the village tavern.

On the old post-road, now called Broadway, going north from the village, Major Andre was captured, and a monument erected on the spot by the people of Westchester County, October 7, 1853, with this inscription:—

ON THIS SPOT,

THE 23D DAY OF SEPTEMBER, 1780, THE SPY,

MAJOR JOHN ANDRE,

Adjutant-General of the British Army, was captured by

JOHN PAULDING, DAVID WILLIAMS, AND ISAAC VAN WART,

ALL NATIVES OF THIS COUNTY.

History has told the rest.

It is said that the tree beneath which Andre was captured was struck by lightning in July, 1801. the very day of Arnold's death in London.

Tarrytown and vicinity was the very heart of the debatable ground of the Revolution; and here, according to Irving, arose the two great orders of border chivalry—the Skinners and the Cow-Boys. The former fought, or rather marauded, under the American, the latter under the British banner. "In the zeal of service both were apt to make blunders, and confounded the property of friend and foe. Neither of them, in the heat and hurry of a foray, had time to ascertain the politics of a horse or cow which they were driving off into captivity, nor

ICHABOD CRANE AND KATRINA VAN TASSEL.

when they wrung the neck of a rooster did they trouble their heads whether he crowed for Congress or King George."

This was indeed an eventful neighborhood to the faithful historian, Diedrich Knickerbocker; and here he picked up many of those legends which were given by him to the world, or found among his papers. One of these was the legend connected with the old Dutch Church of Sleepy Hollow. A drowsy, dreamy influence seems to hang over the land, and to pervade the very atmosphere. "Some say the place was bewitched by a high German doctor during the early days of the settlement; others that an old Indian chief, the wizard of his tribe, held his pow-wows there before Hendrich Hudson's discovery of the river. The dominant spirit, however, that haunts this enchanted region, is the apparition of a figure on horseback without a head, said to be the ghost of a Hessian trooper, and was known at all the country firesides as the "headless horseman" of Sleepy Hollow. Sunnyside, you remember, was once the property of old Baltus Van Tassel; and here lived the fair Katrina, beloved by all the youths, but *more especially* by Ichabod Crane, the country schoolmaster, and a reckless youth, Mr. Van Brunt. A faithful view of the unsuccessful courtship of Ichabod will be seen in the cut here given, from the statuette group of Ichabod and Katrina, by Mr. Rogers, of New York, whose skill we again refer to in our article on "Rip Van Winkle among the Catskills."

The reader will also remember the party one evening, and Ichabod's return; his race with the Headless Horseman, and his disgraceful overthrow. The whole route, and the race for the bridge, recalls the ride of Tam O'Shanter, when pursued by witches on the banks of the Doon. Indeed, the old Dutch Church is not a bad representation of old Alloway Kirk. It was built in the early times of the province, and a tablet over the portal bore the names of its founders—Frederick Phillipsie, patroon of Yonkers, and his wife Katrina Van Cortlandt, of the Van Cortlandt's of Croton, "a powerful family connection, with one foot resting on Spuyten Duyvel and the other on Croton River." In the peaceful burial-yard adjacent sleeps the writer of the gentle heart. A plain slab, with this inscription, marks his resting-place:—

WASHINGTON IRVING,

Born April 3d, 1783. Died November 28th, 1859.

But in the soft summer days and the golden autumn his genius seems to brood over the hills of Tarrytown and Irvington, even as that of

Scott over the valley of the Tweed. The little stream that winds through the valley of Sleepy Hollow is called the Pocantico, an Indian name signifying "dark river."

In a pleasant part of Tarrytown is located the Irving Institute, established in 1838. It is about half a mile from the depot, and commands

IRVING INSTITUTE, TARRYTOWN, N. Y.
Armagnac & Rowe, Principals and Proprietors.

charming views of the Hudson and inland scenery. From its cupola we see, to the south, the Paulding Manor House, the villas of Bierstadt, the Cunningham Castle, Nyack opposite the wide expanse of Tappan Zee, and miles in every direction; and every view has points of historic and poetic interest to every person who has either a taste for history, or legends, which are only the *foliage* of history. It is appropriately styled the "Irving Institute," looking down from its beautiful eminence upon the valley of Sleepy Hollow. We present a fine cut of the building and grounds. It is designed to combine the attractions and *safety* of a home with thoroughness of discipline and intellectual culture.

The Tappan Zee was also supposed to be haunted by the Old Storm Ship, which one evening went up the Hudson and never returned; and also by the "Flying Dutchman," who still rows but never makes a port. Mr. "Van Dam," of graceless memory, attended a quilting frolic at Kakiat, on the opposite shore, one Saturday afternoon; having imbibed rather freely, and danced until midnight, he thought it high time to return. He was warned of the Sabbath's approach, but pulled off, swearing he would not land until he reached Spuyten Duyvel if it took him a month of Sundays. "He was never seen afterward, but may still be heard plying his oars, being the Flying Dutchman of the Tappan Zee, doomed to ply between Kakiat and Spuyten Duyvel until the day of judgment."

NYACK-ON-THE-HUDSON, the pleasant village opposite Tarrytown.

On the western side of the Tappan Zee the mountains sweep back from Piermont in the form of a semi-circle, and meet the river again at the northern extremity of the Zee, in a series of bluffs familiarly known as the Hook, almost as imposing as the Rock of Gibraltar, which it strongly resembles in outline and general appearance. Within this semi-circle—one of the loveliest spots on the river—nestles the village of Nyack, which is rapidly growing into a large suburban town. The Rip Van Winkle sleep which seems to have possessed this part of the western shore of the river from time immemorial, has been very properly disturbed by the extension of the Northern Railway to Nyack, and now all is bustle and activity. No less than three hundred new houses have been erected during the last year. Looking out from the promontory which extends into the "Zee," on a point nearly central between Piermont and the Hook is a stately edifice. This is the Rockland Institute, a college for young ladies, of a high order, which has secured an almost national celebrity. The patrons of the institution are among the most distinguished men of the country in point of wealth and literary eminence; and the varied and attractive features of this institution have drawn students from almost all the principal States of the Union.

The Rev. L. D. Mansfield has been its presiding officer almost from its foundation, and is still at its head. The esteem in which he is held as an educator, may be inferred from the following editorial notice of the Institute, which appeared in a recent copy of the *Journal:*—

"Around the Rockland Female Institute, we venture to say, gather more pleasant associations than cling about any similar institution in the United States. That peculiar love which some men bring to the

ROCKLAND FEMALE INSTITUTE, NYACK-ON-THE-HUDSON.

work in which they are engaged, has been surprisingly and happily illustrated here. Mr. Mansfield, from the very commencement, surrounded himself with an excellent array of teachers in every department, and we assume nothing in saying that to-day the Rockland Female Institute stands in the front rank of all institutions of its kind in the world. This may appear like strong language, but we have said no word which we do not honestly believe to be the truth.

"Grouped about the Institute are many tasteful cottages, a number of which were built by Mr. Mansfield." The whole of this plateau is remarkable for its adaptation to the erection of pleasant country residences, and it is not strange that so many persons of taste, with the means wherewithal to develop and gratify that taste, have chosen it for their abiding-place."

During the long summer vacations, this elegant place is converted into a summer resort, and is known as the Tappan Zee House, under which designation it has attained a deserved popularity. The house contains over sixty rooms, and there are furnished cottages and villas on the grounds. Nyack is peculiarly free from ills which many places are heir to. There is no fever and ague, and *no mosquitos*. The ease of access and the pleasant surroundings make Nyack a desirable place for the summer visitor. Here also, in a pleasant part of the village, within a short distance from the river, is the Smithsonian Hotel, one of the finest home-like hotels for the tourist, summer guest, or transient visitor. It has fine views, healthful location, large and well-furnished rooms. The new ferryboat "Tappan Zee" connects, in the channel, with the day-boats. The old name of Tappan was derived from the Indian name Tup-hanne, signifying Cold Stream.

SING-SING, on the east side, is six miles above Tarrytown, and thirty-two from New York. Its name is said to be derived from the Indian words *ossin*, a stone, and *ing*, a place, from the rocky and stony character of the river bank.

The State Prison, near the river, with its white walls, was built of stone quarried on the spot by a band *o'-sin-ing* mortals imported from Auburn in 1829. For thirty-six years Sing-Sing has also been noted as the great camp-meeting ground of the Methodist Episcopal Church of New York and vicinity.

ROCKLAND LAKE lies opposite Sing-Sing, set in a "dimple of the hills," and is not seen from the river. As we look at the great ice-houses to-day, which, like uncouth barns, stand here and there along the Hudson, it does not seem possible that only a few years ago ice was decidedly unpopular, and wheeled about New York in a hand-cart. Think of one hand-cart supplying New York with ice! It was considered unhealthy, and called forth many learned discussions. The point that *seems* to project into the river was called "Verdietege" Hook, being considered a "very tedious" spot by the old Dutch mariners.

CROTON RIVER meets the Hudson about one mile above Sing-Sing, and it is a singular fact that the *pitcher* and *ice-cooler* of New York, or, in other words, Croton Dam and Rockland Lake, should be directly opposite. About thirty years ago, the Croton first made its appearance in New York, brought in by an aqueduct of solid masonry. The old Indian name of the Croton was Kitch-a-wonck. The Dam is an interesting place to visit, and we understand that city milkmen, when journeying up the river, never pass the point without reverently lifting their hats. We would modestly suggest a yearly picnic to this dam,

LAKE MAHOPAC, ONE OF THE FOUNTAINS OF THE CROTON.

where these modern Hildebrands could worship their "Undines," and compute the value of 500,000,000 gallons at "ten cents a quart,"—a nice little *running account*, large enough per annum to build the State capital or the East River bridge.

LAKE MAHOPAC is one of the finest fountains of the Croton, and the finest lake near the metropolis. It can be reached very easily by the Harlem Railroad-from New York. The old Indian name was Ma-cook-pake, signifying a large inland lake. The same derivation, we imagine, is also seen in Copake Lake, Columbia County. The view here given shows the island where the last meeting of the southern tribes of the Hudson was held. The lake is one thousand feet above tide-water—a magnificent sheet of water, with emerald islands; and it is pleasant to know that the bright waters of Mahopac and the clear fountains of Putnam County are carried to New York, even as the poetic waters of Loch Katrine supply the commercial city of Glasgow. Lake Mahopac has fine hotels, and is a pleasant place of summer resort.

TELLER'S POINT was called by the Indians, Senasqua; and tradition says that the ancient warriors still haunt the surrounding glens and woods, and the sachems of Teller's Point are household words in the neighborhood. It is also said that there was once a great Indian battle here, and perhaps the ghosts of the old warriors are attracted by the Underhill Grapery and the 10,000 gallons of wine bottled every year.

HAVERSTRAW BAY.—Passing Teller's Point we come into Haverstraw Bay. This expanse of water was called by the Indians, Kumachenack. The village is on the west side. Three miles above Haverstraw, also on the west side, we pass Stony Point, where, at two o'clock one morning, Wayne—better known as "Mad Anthony"—sent the brief despatch to Washington: "Dear General—The American flag waves here." Passing Verplank's Point, just opposite Stony Point, and we see

PEEKSKILL, forty-three miles from New York, on the east bank, where Nathan Palmer, the spy, was hung; and another brief message sent by Putnam, to the effect, "Nathan Palmer was taken as a spy, tried as a spy, and will be hanged as a spy.—P. S. *He is hanged.*" In 1797 Peekskill was the headquarters of old Israel Putnam. This was the birthplace of Paulding, one of Andre's captors, and he died here in 1818. There is a monument to his memory about two miles north of the village. It is said that the stream and town took their names from a worthy Dutch skipper, Jans Peek, who imagined he had found the head waters of the Hudson, and run aground, on the east side, in the stream which now bears his name. It was called by the Indians the unpoetic name Sackboes. Near Peekskill is the old Van Cortlandt house, the residence of Washington for a short time during the Revolution. East of the village is the farm and summer home of the great pulpit-orator of our country—Henry Ward Beecher.

THE HIGHLANDS — SUBLIMITY.

"And ever-wakeful Echo here doth dwell,
The nymph of sportive mockery, that still
Hides behind every rock, in every dell,
And softly glides unseen from hill to hill."

Turning Kidd's Point, or Caldwell's Landing, almost at right angles, the steamer enters the Highlands. Near the Point will be seen some upright planks, or caissons, near the water's edge. They mark the spot where Captain Kidd's ship was supposed to have been scuttled. As the famous captain's history seems to be quite intimately associated with the Hudson, we will give in brief

THE STORY OF CAPTAIN KIDD.—His name was William, and he was born about the middle of the seventeenth century; and it is thought, near Greenock, in Scotland: resided at one time in New York, near the corner of William and Cedar Streets, and was there married. In April, 1696, Kidd sailed from England in command of the "Adventure Galley," with full armament and eighty men. He captured a French ship, and, on arrival at New York, put up articles for volunteers: remained in New York three or four months, increasing his crew to one hundred and fifty-five men, and sailed thence to Maderas, thence to Bonavista and St. Jago, to Madagascar, then to Calicut, then to Madagascar again, then sailed and took the "Quedah Merchant." Kidd kept forty shares of the spoils, and divided the rest with his crew. He then burned the "Adventure Galley," went on board the "Quedah Merchant," and sailed for the West Indies. Here he left the "Merchant," with part of the crew, under one Bolton, as commander. Then manned a sloop, and taking part of his spoils, went to Boston via Long Island Sound, and is said to have set goods on shore at different places. In the mean time, in August, 1698, the East India Company informed the Lords Justices that Kidd had committed several acts of piracy, particularly in seizing a Moor's ship called the "Quedah Merchant." When Kidd landed at Boston he was therefore arrested by the Earl of Bellamont, and sent to England for trial, 1699, where he was found guilty and executed. Now it is supposed that the crew of the "Quedah

Merchant," which Kidd left at Hispaniola, started with their ship for the Hudson, as the crew was mostly gathered from the Highlands and above It is said that they passed New York in the night, and started with their ship for the manor of Livingston; but encountering a gale in the Highlands, and thinking they were pursued, run her near the shore, now known as Kidd's Point, and here scuttled her, and the crew fled to the woods with such treasure as they could carry. Whether this circumstance was true or not, it was at least a current story in the neighborhood, and an enterprising individual, about forty years ago, *caused an old cannon* to be discovered in the river, and perpetrated the first "Cardiff Giant Hoax." A New York Stock Company was organized to prosecute the work. It was said that the ship could be seen in clear days, with her masts still standing, many fathoms below the surface. One thing is certain—the Company didn't see it or the *treasurer* either, in whose hands were deposited about $30,000.

THE DUNDERBERG rises directly above this point—the Olympus of Dutch Mythology. It was the dread of the early navigators, and sailors had to drop the peaks of their mainsails in salute to the goblin who inhabited it, and presided over those little imps in sugar-loaf hats and short doublets, who were frequently seen tumbling head over heels in the rack and mist. No wonder that the old burghers of New York never thought of making their week's voyage to Albany without arranging their wills; and it created as much commotion in New Amsterdam as a Stanley expedition in search of Livingstone. Verdrietege Hook, the Dunderberg, and the Overslaugh were names of terror to even the bravest skipper.

ANTHONY'S NOSE.—The high peak on the east bank, just above the "Nameless Highland," is Anthony's Nose, which, in our Guide-Book published in 1869, we considered the prominent *feature* of the Hudson. It is about 1500 feet high, and has two or three *christenings*. One says it was named after St. Anthony the Great—the first institutor of monastic life, born A.D. 251, at Coma, in Heraclea, a town in Upper Egypt. Irving's humorous account is, however, quite as probable, to wit: that it was *derived* from the nose of Anthony Van Corlear, the illustrious trumpeter of Peter Stuyvesant. "Now thus it happened that bright and early in the morning the good Anthony, having washed his burly visage, was leaning over the quarter-railing of the galley, contemplating it in the glassy waves below. Just at this moment the illustrious sun, breaking in all his splendor from behind a high bluff of the Highlands, did dart one of his most potent beams full upon the refulgent *nose* of the sounder of brass, the reflection of which shot straightway down hissing hot into the water, and killed a mighty sturgeon that was sporting beside the vessel. When this astonishing miracle was made known to the Governor, and he tasted of the unknown fish, he marveled exceedingly; and, as a monument thereof, he gave the name of Anthony's Nose to a stout promontory in the neighborhood, and it has continued to be called Anthony's Nose ever since." This mountain was called by the Indians Kittatenny, a Delaware term signifying "endless hills."

Opposite Anthony's Nose is the beautiful island of Iona; and we obtain a fine view of old Sugar-Loaf to the north. We are now in the midst of historic country, and the various points are literally crowded together: Beverley Dock, Beverley House, Fort Putnam, North and South Redoubt Mountains, Kosciusko's Garden, and Fort Constitution. Both sides of the river are full of interest, and we will refer to each separately. As the steamer is now nearing the west shore, we will speak first of

WEST POINT.—The large building on the rock is Cozzens' Hotel, and the anding near is known as Cozzens' Dock. Buttermilk Falls, a little south of the landing, was known among the Indians as the Prince's Falls, owned by a prince of the hill country. The rivulet south of these falls was called by the Indians the Ossinapink, or the stream from the solid rocks; and the stream below Anthony's Nose, on the east side, the Brocken Kill, a Dutch word from water *broken* into waterfalls. The next landing is about one mile above Cozzens', and is the proper West Point Landing.

Washington first suggested this place as the most eligible situation for a military academy. It went into operation about 1812, and the land was ceded to the General Government of the United States in the year 1826. The Academy Buildings and Parade Ground are on a fine plateau about two hundred feet above the river. The parade-ground seems almost as level as a floor; and, as the buildings are at a little distance from the river, they are only partially seen. The first building on the right hand to one ascending from the landing is the riding-school used in winter. To the rear of this the public stables, accommodating one hundred and fifty horses. Then, as you ascend, the pathway brings you to a new fireproof building for offices, a beautiful feature. To the right hand of this building is the library, with a dome. The next building is the chapel; and next to the chapel is the old riding-hall, now used for recitation-rooms, gymnasiums, gallery of paintings, and museums. On the same street are located the cadet barracks; and to the north, the officers' quarters. Prominent in this vicinity is the fine monument to General Sedgwick. Starting again at the old riding-hall, and going south, we come to the cadet hall and the cadet hospital; and still further south, another section of officers' quarters. Near the flag-staff will be found a fine collection of old cannon, old chains, old shell, and the famous "swamp angel" gun, taken from the rebels. Fort Knox was just above the landing. Near the river bank can also be seen Dade's Monument, Kosciusko's Garden, and Kosciusko's Monument. Old Fort Clinton was located on the plain, near the monument; and far above, like a sentinel left at his post, Fort Putnam looks down upon the changes of a hundred years. But of all places around West Point, Kosciusko's Garden seems the finest and most suggestive, connected as it is with a hero not only of his own country, but a man ready to battle for free institutions, taking up the sublime words of the old Roman orator, "Where *Liberty* is, *there* is my country." A beautiful spring is near the Garden, and the indenture of a cannon-ball is still pointed out in the rocks, which must have disturbed the patriot's meditations.

West Point during the Revolution was the Gibraltar of the Hudson; and the saddest lesson of those stern old days is connected with its history. Benedict Arnold was in command of this important point, and the story of his treachery is familiar to every schoolboy. It will be remembered that Arnold met Andre at the house of Joshua Hett Smith, at a place now known as Treason Hill, near the village of Haverstraw. Major Andre was sent as the representative of the British commander,

Sir Henry Clinton. Andre, with the papers and plans of Arnold secreted in his *boots*, passes down the Tarrytown road, and was arrested, as we said in our article on Tarrytown, and the papers discovered. With this preface, our history will carry us across the river to

GARRISON, on the east side. Arnold returned from Haverstraw to the Beverley House, where he was then living. This house is situated about one mile south of the Garrison Depot, near the magnificent grounds and residence of the Hon. Hamilton Fish. Colonel Jamieson sent a letter to Arnold informing him of the facts, and this letter Arnold received on the morning of the 24th of September. Alexander Hamilton and General Lafayette were at breakfast with him. He read its contents and excused himself from the table, kissed his wife good-bye, told her he was a ruined man and a traitor, kissed his little boy in the cradle, fled to Beverley Dock, and ordered his men to pull off and go down the river. The "Vulture," English man-of-war, was near Teller's Point, and received a traitor, whose living treason had to be atoned by the blood of Andre, the noble and pure-hearted officer. It is said that Arnold lived long enough to be hissed in the House of Commons, as he once took his seat in the gallery, and he died friendless, and, in fact, despised. It is also said that one day when Talleyrand arrived in Havre on foot from Paris, in the darkest hour of the French Revolution, pursued by the bloodhounds of the reign of terror, he was about to secure a passage to the United States, and asked the landlord of the hotel, "So there are Americans staying at your house? I am going across the water, and would like a letter to a person of influence in the New World." "There is a gentleman up-stairs from Britain or America," was the response. He pointed the way, and Talleyrand ascended the stairs. In a dimly lighted room sat the man of whom the great minister of France was to ask a favor. He advanced, and poured forth in elegant French and broken English, "I am a wanderer, and an exile. I am forced to fly to the New World without a friend or home. You are an American. Give me, then, I beseech you, a letter of yours, so that I may be able to earn my bread." The strange gentleman rose. With a look that Talleyrand never forgot, he retreated toward the door of the next chamber. He spoke as he retreated, and his voice was full of

41

suffering: "I am the only man of the New World who can raise his hand to God and say, 'I have not a friend, not one, in America!'" "Who are you?" he cried. "Your name?" "My name is Benedict Arnold." Would that our modern traitors had the same vulture at their vitals as in the early days of the Republic, when treason was made odious without the aid of politicians.

If West Point and its fortifications had passed at that time into the hands of the enemy, it would be difficult to say what disaster might have befallen our arms; but, through all those dark days, when the

THE HIGHLAND HOUSE, GARRISON, N. Y.
G. F. & W. D. GARRISON, Proprietors and owners.

American army literally tracked their way with blood through the snows of seven winters, it seemed as if the matter was entirely in the hands of Divine Providence; and that the words of Patrick Henry were every day verified: "There is a just God, who presides over the destinies of nations."

As we have before stated, the station Garrison, on the Hudson River Railroad, is directly opposite West Point, and about half a mile from the depot is the Highland House, standing on a magnificent plateau.

We call attention to the fact that this is *not* the Highland House near Cozzen's, neither is it the little house at the ferry crossing, as unpleasant mistakes have sometimes been made, but "The Highland House," about four hundred feet above the river, appropriately named, lying in the very centre of the Highlands. Its proprietors are descendants of the family who lived here in the time of the Revolution, from whom the ferry and landing took their name. The house has been recently enlarged to almost double its former capacity. Its location is certainly

INDIAN FALLS, NEAR HIGHLAND HOUSE, GARRISON, N. Y.

one of the finest along the river. The plateau is inclosed by the North Redoubt and South Redoubt Mountains, reaching from Sugar-Loaf and Anthony's Nose on the south, to Breakneck on the north.

Wander where you will, the surrounding mountains abound with wild and picturesque glens. Poet, artist, novelist, and historian, *all* who find books in running brooks, continually add their testimony to the accumulating evidence. In brief, all who wish to spend a summer pleasantly and profitably will find the "Highland House"—a cut of which is here given—one of the finest family hotels on the Hudson River. Its location is picturesque and healthy, on higher ground than West Point, and commanding a full view. The scenery and drives of the Highlands are very fine.

About a mile and a half to the north, in a picturesque glen, are Indian Falls, well known to artists, and by them made familiar to those who never had the opportunity of visiting one of the prettiest little points of scenery on the Hudson. It is impossible to condense their beauty into a single sketch, but we present the above cut as an index-hand pointing the tourist to the real beauty of which any representation would be only a shadow. With a book of poems in hand, or a *walking romance* on one's arm, we imagine a summer's day would glide by, "as golden hours on angel wings."

The Glen Falls are only half a mile distant; and, added to this blended history and beauty, all over this eastern bank there are local legends—unclaimed children of history—waiting for their relationship to be acknowledged. Surely there is no place where the history of our country can be studied with greater interest than among these wild fastnesses, where Freedom found protection.

CONSTITUTION POINT.—A short distance above West Point Landing the steamer turns a right angle. On the east bank, almost opposite, known as Constitution Island, lives Miss Susan Warner, author of "Queechy" and "The Wide, Wide World," of which latter work 40,000 copies were sold in the United States. On this point, or island, ruins of the old fort are still seen. It was once called Martalaer's Rock Island.

COLD SPRING.—A little to the north, also on east bank, is the village of Cold Spring, which received its name very naturally from the fact that there *was* a cold spring in the vicinity. A short distance north of the village we see

UNDERCLIFF, the home of the poet Morris, now owned by his son. It lies, in fact, *under the cliff* and shadow of Mount Taurus, and has a fine outlook upon the river and surrounding mountains. Standing on the piazza, we see directly in front of us Old Cro' Nest; and it was on this piazza that the poet wrote

"Where Hudson's wave o'er silvery sands
Winds through the hills afar,
Old Cro' Nest like a monarch stands,
Crowned with a single star."

OLD CRO' NEST.
(From Lossing's "Hudson, from the Wilderness to the Sea.")

It is said that Mrs. Morris was the *original* of that beautiful character painted by Washington Irving, in his charming essay, "The Wife."

OLD CRO' NEST is the first mountain above West Point, and 1418 feet high. Its name was given from a circular lake on the summit, suggesting by its form and solitary location a nest among the mountains, and this fancy soon gave a name to the entire mountain. This mountain is also intimately associated with poetry, as the scene of Rodman Drake's "Culprit Fay":—

> "'Tis the middle watch of a summer night,
> The earth is dark, but the heavens are bright,
> The moon looks down on Old Cro' Nest—
> She mellows the shade on his shaggy breast,
> And seems his huge grey form to throw
> In a silver cone on the wave below."

STORM KING, to the north of Cro' Nest, is the highest peak of the Highlands, being 1800 feet above tide water. Its first name was Klinkersberg, afterward called Butter Hill, and christened by Willis Storm King. This mountain forms the northern portal of the Highlands, on the west side. Breakneck is opposite, on the east side, where St. Anthony's Face was blasted away. In this mountain solitude there was a shade of reason in giving that solemn countenance of stone the name of St. Anthony, as a good representation of monastic life; and, by a quiet sarcasm, the full-length nose below was probably thus suggested.

The Highlands now trend off to the northeast, and we see the New Beacon, or Grand Sachem Mountain, 1685 feet high, and about half a mile to the north, the Old Beacon, 1471 feet in height. These mountains were used for signal stations during the Revolution. They were called by the Indians the Matteawan, and the whole range of Highlands were sometimes referred to as the Wequehachke, or the Hill Country. It was also believed by the Indians that, in ancient days, "before the Hudson poured its waters from the lakes, the Highlands formed one vast prison, within whose rocky bosom the omnipotent Manito confined the rebellious spirits who repined at his control. Here, bound in adamantine chains, or jammed in rifted pines, or crushed by ponderous rocks, they groaned for many an age. At length the conquering Hudson, in its career toward the ocean, burst open their prison-house, rolling its tide triumphantly through the stupendous ruins." An idea quite in accordance with modern science.

The steamer is now passing close to the base of old Storm King, and we get a fine view of this mountain rock, with sides all scarred and torn by storms and lightning. Almost before us, to the right, we see

POLLIPEL'S ISLAND, supposed by the Indians to be a supernatural

UPPER ENTRANCE TO THE HIGHLANDS, FROM CORNWALL LANDING.

(From Lossing's "Hudson, from the Wilderness to the Sea.")

spot. The island, however, has a little romance connected with it, which is decidedly *supernatural*. Some fair Katrina of the neighborhood, a great many years ago, was beloved by a farmer's lad. She reciprocates, but, by coquettish art, was playing the —— (sad havoc) with a young minister's affections. One winter evening, minister and Katrina were driving on the ice, near this island. The farmer's son very naturally was also driving in the same vicinity. The ice broke, and minister and young lady were rescued by the bold youth. The minister discovers that Katrina and young Hendrich both love each other; and there, under the moonlight, on that supernatural island, with solemn ceremony, unites them in bonds of holy matrimony. It ought henceforth and forever to be called the "Lovers' Island." This pleasing story presents a strong contrast to the sad fate of a wedding-party at the Danskammer Rock, to which we shortly refer. We are now nearing the pleasant village of

CORNWALL, where the hillsides are crowned with villas and summer homes. This is one of the pleasantest and healthiest places on the Hudson. A short distance from the village, on the old road leading from Cornwall to Newburgh, is situated Idlewild, where Willis passed the last fifteen years of his life; and now, as the steamer leaves Cornwall Landing, we are in the beautiful *bay of Newburgh*, pronounced by many the finest point on the Hudson.

NEWBURGH—settled by the Palatines, 1708. As we approach Newburgh, on the west bank, we see the old house known as Washington's Headquarters, already noticed in our *analysis* of the river. Here are gathered, as we stated in our Guide for 1869, many relics of the Revolution: old Hessian boots that were never intended for flight, making either victory or capture inevitable; old swords that have a history written in blood; trappings of soldiers, that have lost the glitter and the tinsel; and a piano of most harmonious discord.

At the time of disbanding the army Congress was negligent in furnishing supplies or payment; the soldiers wished to make Washington the head of a monarchical government; he declined; then an appeal was secretly disseminated to officers to form a military despotism. Washington was informed of it. He called a meeting of the soldiers, on the grounds near the old building, and his first words, before unfolding the paper, touched every heart. "You see, gentlemen," said he, as he placed his spectacles before his eyes, "that I have not only grown gray but blind in your service." It is needless to say that the mutiny was quelled. If the logic of war has not been sufficient to answer the old argument of State Rights, it would be well to re-read the history of those disjointed days, and see if there were not previous to our Constitution sufficient need to "form a more perfect union."

The city rises in natural terraces, and presents a fine river front. It is the eastern terminus of the *Newburgh Branch* of the *Erie Railway*.

FISHKILL LANDING.—Opposite Newburgh are the villages of Matteawan and Fishkill; and about one mile to the south, the depot and ferry of the *Duchess and Columbia Railroad*, which connects with the Connecticut Western, and makes a direct eastern route to Hartford and Boston. These thriving towns guard the northern portal of the Highlands, sixty miles from New York.

We will close our third division of the Hudson with a few verses from a little poem which revives in happy music the ringing of the Hudson sleigh-bells, as they once rang out their music under these grand old mountains. Our moonlight picture will at once call up to every one some little experience of their far-off days.

HUDSON SLEIGH-BELLS.

With sweetheart nestled close by our side,
We were started off for a jolly ride—
    With a sleighing party.

When we were young, with nothing to do
But busy ourselves at trying to woo
The girl who had stolen our boyish heart;
The little coquette! how she played her part
    At that sleighing party.

Away we glide, with mirth and glee,
Joyous and happy as youth can be,—
While the sweet and merry music swells
From happy hearts and tuneful bells
      Of the sleighing party.

The snow falls faster!—so she said,
Tossing her curls and dropping her head
Till the tinted cheeks were totally hid.
I couldn't resist—she didn't forbid—
      'Twas a sleighing party.

      Protect her! Of course!
The snow was blinding, the air was keen;
As I drew her closer it could not have been
That the red-ripe lips, so tempting to kiss,
And those tell-tale eyes meant other than Yes!
      At a sleighing party.

Didn't I kiss her?
But why you should laugh I never could tell,
For I know you boys would have liked it well;
And as to the girls, they all well knew
That the unkissed ones were very few
      At that sleighing party.

We trust that we will find sympathy among our readers for this suggestion of star-lit eyes; and, in the summer season, we consider these snow-scenes as a species of ice-cream dessert.

HILLSIDES FOR TWENTY MILES—THE PICTURESQUE.

> "By woody bluff we steal, by leaning lawn,
> By palace, village, cot,—a sweet surprise
> At every turn the vision breaks upon."

Low Point, or Carthage, is a small village on the east bank, about four miles north of Fishkill. It was called by the early inhabitants Low Point, as New Hamburgh, two miles to the north, was called High Point. Almost opposite Low Point, on the west bank, is a large flat rock, covered with cedars, known as the

Duyvel's Dans Kammer.—Here Hendrich Hudson, in his voyage up the river, witnessed an Indian pow-wow—the first recorded fireworks in a country which has since delighted in rockets and pyrotechnic displays. Here, too, in later years, tradition relates the sad fate of a wedding-party. It seems that a Mr. Hans Hansen and a Miss Katrina Van Voorman, with a few friends, were returning from Albany, and disregarding the old Indian prophecy, were all slain:—

> "For none that visit the Indian's den,
> Return again to the haunts of men;
> The knife is their doom! O sad is their lot!
> Beware, beware of the blood-stained spot!"

Some years ago this spot was also searched for the buried treasures of Captain Kidd, and we know of one river pilot who still dreams semi-yearly of there finding countless chests of gold.

Two miles above, on the east side, we pass New Hamburgh, at the mouth of Wappinger's Creek. The name Wappinger had its origin from Wabun, east, and Acki, land. This tribe held the east bank of the river, from Manhattan to Roeliffe Jansen's Creek, which empties into the Hudson near Livingston, a few miles south of Catskill Station on the Hudson River Railroad. Passing the little villages of Hampton, Marlborough, and Milton, on the west bank, and we see on the east bank,

Locust Grove, residence of the late Prof. S. F. B. Morse, inventor of the electric telegraph, who for all time will receive the congratulations of every civilized nation, and the whole globe is destined one day to speak *his* language. Yes, the islands of the sea, and the people that sit afar off in darkness, are beginning to feel the pulses of the world through the "still small voice" whispering beneath ocean and river, and across mighty continents, "putting a girdle round the earth in forty minutes," like the fairy of *Midsummer-Night's Dream*.

We now see Blue Point, on the west bank; and, in every direction, we have the finest views. The scenery seems to stand, in character, between the sublimity of the Highlands and the tranquil dreamy repose of the Tappan Zee. It is said that under the shadow of these hills was the favorite anchorage of

The Storm Ship, one of our oldest and therefore most reliable legends. The story runs somewhat as follows. Years ago, when New York was a village—a mere cluster of houses on the point now known as the Battery—when the Bowery was the farm of Peter Stuyvesant, and the Old Dutch Church on Nassau Street (now used as the post-office) was considered the country—when communication with the old world was semi-yearly instead of semi-weekly or daily—say one hundred and fifty years ago—the whole town one evening was put into great commotion by the fact that a ship was coming up the bay. She approached the Battery within hailing distance, and then, sailing against both wind and tide, turned aside and passed up the Hudson. Week after week and month after month elapsed, but she never returned; and whenever a storm came down on Haverstraw Bay or Tappan Zee, it is said that she could be seen careening over the waste; and, in the midst of the turmoil, you could hear the captain giving orders, in *good Low Dutch;* but when the weather was pleasant, her favorite anchorage was among the shadows of the picturesque hills, on the eastern bank, a few miles above the Highlands. It was thought by some to be Hendrich Hudson and his crew of the "Half Moon," who, it was well known, had once run aground in the upper part of the river, seeking a northwest passage to China; and people who live in this vicinity still insist that under the calm harvest moon and the pleasant nights of September, they see her under the bluff of Blue Point, all in deep shadow, save her topsails glittering in the moonlight. Perhaps it was this quiet anchorage that gave the name to

POUGHKEEPSIE, Queen City of the Hudson,—derived from the Indian word Apokeepsing, signifying safe harbor. Near the landing is a bold rock jutting into the river, known as Kaal Rock, signifying barren rock; and perhaps this also furnished a safe harbor or landing-place for those days of birch canoes. It is said there are over forty different ways of spelling Poughkeepsie, and every year the Post-Office Record gives a new one. The first house was built in 1702 by a Mr. Van Kleek; and we believe the State Legislature held a session here in 1777 or 1778, when New York was held by the British, and Kingston had been burned by Vaughn. Ten years later, the State Convention also met here for ratification of the Federal Constitution. (For further historical particulars see Barber's Historical Collection of New York, or the State Records.) The city has a beautiful location, and is justly regarded the finest residence city on the river; and it is not only midway between New York and Albany, but it is also bounded by a historic and poetic horizon midway between the Highlands and the Catskills, commanding a view of the mountain portals on the south and the mountain overlook on the north—the Gibraltar of Revolutionary fame and the dreamland of Rip Van Winkle. The magnificent steamers which ply daily between New York and Albany, thirty trains on the best-appointed railroad in the country, and fine steamers of home enterprise, make the traveling facilities complete. The city has a population of 25,000 inhabitants— the largest between the capital and the metropolis. In addition to its natural beauty, Poughkeepsie is noted throughout our country for refined society, and as a nucleus of the finest schools in our country.

Just before the river boats land at Poughkeepsie we see upon our right, as we come up the river, a large structure, the "Riverview Military Academy." It crowns a fine eminence looking off toward the Highlands on the south, and the Catskills to the north and west. It is most thoroughly ventilated, and heated by steam throughout. Water is accessible on every floor, and the room of each pupil is pleasant and commodious. The views are delightful in every direction, as will be seen from the cut here given. Mr. Bisbee has met with the most marked success in training boys for business, college, for West Point, and other military and naval institutions. In fact, he believes in an education which results in *force* of character—the true aim of all education.

RIVERVIEW MILITARY ACADEMY.

A wide-awake thorough-going School for Boys wishing to be trained for Business, for College, or for West Point or the Naval Academy.

OTIS BISBEE, A. M., PRINCIPAL AND PROPRIETOR.

We would also mention "Vassar College" and "Poughkeepsie Female Academy," the latter under the rectorship of the Rev. D. G. Wright, A.M. It is located in the central part of the city, and has long been distinguished for its thoroughness of instruction and carefulness of supervision. The buildings are ample and commodious; the rooms large, well ventilated, and furnished with regard to taste, convenience,

(RESIDENCE OF THE HON. H. G. EASTMAN.)

These Grounds are appropriately styled the "Central Park" of Poughkeepsie.

and home comfort. The laboratory is furnished with an extensive philosophical, chemical, and astronomical apparatus. Pupils are carried through a collegiate course, or fitted to enter any class in Vassar College. For many years this Academy has ranked among the first in our State in educational spirit and progress; and there are few, if any, places where young ladies acquire a more healthy mental or moral education, a more finished and perfect symmetry in the development of mind and heart. We present a cut of the Academy on the opposite page.

Vassar College, situated two miles from the City Hall, ranks among the first educational institutions of our land. It is for young ladies what Yale and Harvard are for young men. It was founded by the late Matthew Vassar, who has left behind him, in this stately building and generous endowment, "a monument more lasting than brass." We regret that we have not a cut of the buildings and grounds, and hope to secure them another season.

Near the river landing we see the extensive manufactory of Adriance, Platt, & Co. In 1857 and 1858 this firm commenced the manufacture and sale of the Buckeye Mower at Poughkeepsie, with salesroom in New York. The business has increased and enlarged in their hands materially, and they have attained such excellence in the manufacture of their machines that their reputation is world-wide. Twelve years have sufficed to extend the sale of the Buckeye from twenty-five machines to 30,000 in a single season. Surely the old chariots of war have become chariots of peace.

The fine park, grounds and terrace buildings of Mayor Eastman are a fine feature of the city. The new terrace building is, taken with the entire surroundings, the finest on the Hudson, or any other river in the world. He has been a live man in the city, and has always stood in the front rank of enterprise. His grounds are always open to the public. The houses of his Terrace Block are now completed, and can be purchased for what the rent of an ordinary house in the city of New York would cost for only three or four years. His Business College, referred to in another place, is a very successful institution, and its reputation reaches, like the Pacific Railroad, from New York to San

POUGHKEEPSIE FEMALE ACADEMY.

Francisco. In fact, we know of no city that has been so thoroughly advertised as Poughkeepsie, through its various institutions and successful enterprise.

The "Morgan House," a cut of which is here given, is a fine hotel, situated in the central part of the city, corner of Main and Catherine

MORGAN HOUSE, POUGHKEEPSIE, N. Y.
L. S. PUTNAM, Proprietor.

Streets. Carriages meet the boats and cars. The horse-cars also pass the door. It is considered the finest city hotel between New York and Albany. L. S. Putnam, Proprietor.

The Memorial Fountain, "To the Patriot Dead of Duchess County," is probably the finest in the State; the Collingwood Opera-House is an elegant music-hall capable of seating twenty-two hundred people; the Insane Asylum is a magnificent structure; and the drives are charming in every direction. In fact, it would be an easy matter to write a work on Poughkeepsie alone; and we would like to write fifteen or twenty pages on the

POUGHKEEPSIE AND EASTERN RAILROAD, which forms a direct route across the county, connecting the pleasant valley of the Harlem and the Housatonic with the Hudson. We would suggest, as one of the finest little trips out of New York, the day boat to Poughkeepsie; spend a day in the city; take the Poughkeepsie and Eastern Railroad to Millerton; run up to Bash-Bish Falls, near Copake, or down the Harlem to the Dover Stone Church, to Lake Mahopac, and so to New York,—making the whole trip in three days. This route also, in connection with the Connecticut Western, opens up a direct way to Hartford and Boston. We would also like to speak of the enterprise of the city in supplying pure water from the Hudson; and the coming bridge, connecting the east with the coal-fields of Pennsylvania.

As the steamer leaves Poughkeepsie, we see New Paltz Landing, almost opposite, and Hyde Park, on east bank, six miles above Poughkeepsie. Then Staatsburgh Station, on the east side; and then Rhinebeck, ninety miles from New York. Rondout, or City of Kingston, is directly opposite, at the mouth of Rondout Creek. This is the eastern end of the Delaware and Hudson Canal. Rhinebeck is two miles from Rhinecliff Landing, and is one of the finest towns in Duchess County. It was named, as some say, by combining two words—Beckman and Rhine. Others say that the word *beek* means cliff, and the town was so named from the resemblance of the cliffs to those of the Rhine.

RONDOUT had its derivation from the redoubt that was built on the banks of the creek. The creek took the name of Redoubt Kill, afterward Rundout, and then Rondout. The old town of Kingston was once called Esopus, on Esopus Creek, which flows north and empties into the Hudson at Saugerties.

THE NEW YORK, KINGSTON, AND SYRACUSE RAILROAD has its eastern terminus at Rondout. It passes west through Kingston, West Hurley,

Shokan, Big Indian, crosses the Catskill Mountains to Dean's Corners, and so o Stamford. It runs through a romantic country, and the trip over the mountains is very fine. At West Hurley, only nine miles from Rondout, stages connect for the Overlook Mountain House, a fine hotel 3,800 feet above the river. The hotel is two hundred feet long,

OVERLOOK MOUNTAIN HOUSE.

J. E. LASHER, Proprietor.

Ninety miles from New York, sixty miles from Albany.

and three stories high, commanding a valley view of more than a hundred miles,—while mountains without number rise on every hand, the named and the nameless, from High Point in the southwest to Mount Holyoke in the east.

THE CATSKILLS—BEAUTY.

"And soon the Catskills print the distant sky,
And o'er their airy tops the faint clouds driven,
So softly blending that the cheated eye
Now questions which is earth or which is heaven."

We have now approached the fifth division of our river, guarded by the most classic range of mountains in our country. By a *natural ascendancy* they have many counties of the Hudson under their jurisdiction—Ulster, Greene, and Albany, on the west bank; and Duchess, Columbia, and Rensselaer, on the east.

The first place above Rhinecliff, our last landing, is the village of BARRYTOWN, on the east bank, ninety-six miles from New York. It is said, when Jackson was President, and this village wanted a post-office, that he would not allow it under the name of Barrytown, from personal dislike to General Barry, and suggested another name. But the people were loyal to their old friend, and *went without* a post-office until a new administration. The name Barrytown, therefore, stands as a monument to pluck. The place is known among the old settlers as Lower Red Hook Landing.

TIVOLI, one hundred miles from New York, is the only name on our river that ought to be printed in old-style Roman letters, for it carries us back to the days of the Seven-Hilled City, and one of the famous watering-places of the days of Horace. We have sometimes thought it received its name from a little waterfall near the landing and its general romantic surroundings. One of the mansions of the old Livingston family is near the village. Saugerties lies directly opposite.

GERMANTOWN, 105 miles from New York, is on the east side. A short distance above, the Roeliffe Jansens Kill flows into the Hudson. This stream, called by the Indians the Sankpenak, was the boundary between the Wappingers on the south and the Mohegans on the north. Near its mouth is the old Claremont estate—the original Livingston manor. Here Fulton's project found special favor, and he was materially aided by the sympathy and generosity of Chancellor Livingston. The first steamboat on the Hudson made its first trip the early part of September,

1807, and was called the "Claremont," as a testimonial of gratitude. The trip from New York to Albany, in those "good old days," took *about* forty hours (*vide* Lossing's "Wilderness to the Sea.")

CATSKILL LANDING is just above the mouth of the Catskill, or Kauterskill Creek. It is said that the creek and mountains took their name from the following fact. It is known that each tribe had a *totemic* emblem, or rude banner: the Mohegans had the wolf as their emblem, and some say, that the word Mohegan means the enchanted wolf. (The Lenni Lenapes, or Delawares, at the Highlands, had the turkey as their totem.) Catskill was the southern boundary of the Mohegans on the west bank, and here they set up their emblem. It is said, from this fact the stream took the name of the Kaaters-kill. The large cat and wolf were at least similar in appearance, from the mark of King Aepgin in his deed to Van Rensselaer. Perhaps, however, the mountains at one time abounded in these animals, and the emblem may be only a coincidence.

PROSPECT PARK HOTEL.—The first thing that attracts our attention as the steamer nears the landing, is a fine hotel, well known to the public through a successful three years' administration—the Prospect Park Hotel: Jno. Breasted, Proprietor. This plateau, two hundred and fifty feet above the river, is appropriately named; for, as you sit on the broad piazza which almost surrounds the hotel, you can see to the south, the valley of the Hudson for thirty miles—the "Man in the Mountain," and the whole range of the Catskills; to the north and northeast, the Green Mountains of Vermont, and whichever way you look, it seems as if the river lay at your feet. The grounds are seventeen acres in extent, and are well adapted to the chief design. Guests can find either shade, sunshine, or quiet. It was first opened in 1870, and within these three years the proprietor has been compelled to enlarge it to more than double its former capacity. The main building is now two hundred and fifty feet front, with wing one hundred and fifty feet by forty. There are three hundred and seventy feet of two-storied piazza, sixteen feet wide, supported by Corinthian pillars twenty-five feet high. We think it is safe to say that it is the most airy and cheer-

PROSPECT PARK HOTEL,
CATSKILL, NEW YORK.

ful hotel on the river bank between New York and Albany. Like Aladdin's Palace it sprung up all at once, white and beautiful, and gave life, as it were, to the whole landscape. It is one of the few hotels that had the good fortune to become prominent all at once; and this popularity was not accidental, but owing to many causes: its fine location—its enchanting views—its splendid management. Moreover, the fresh bracing air from the Catskills makes Catskill one of the pleasantest places to spend the heat of the summer, or the noontide of the year;

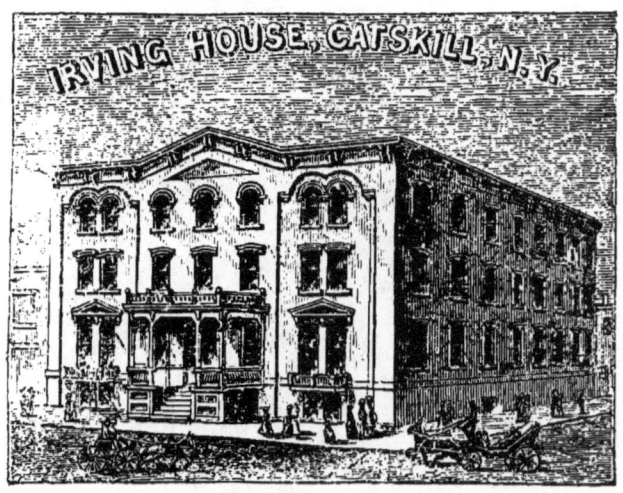

IRVING HOUSE.
H. A. PENSON, Proprietor.

and, indeed, a summer tour is not complete unless we pay Catskill a visit. Prospect Park stages and carriages meet passengers at the landing.

CATSKILL VILLAGE.—The old village, with its Main Street, lies along the valley of the Catskill Creek, not quite a mile from the Causeway Landing, and preserves some of the features of the days when *Knickerbocker* was accustomed to pay it an annual visit. Its location seems to have been chosen as a place of security—out of sight to one voyaging up the river. It has, however, grown rapidly during the last few years, and the northern slope is covered with fine residences, all of which command extensive views of the Hudson. A new hotel, long needed in the business part of the village, was built on Main Street in 1871. It was appropriately christened the "Irving House," as Catskill owes a large part of its present popularity—probably more than it imagines—to the pen of Washington Irving. It is fitted up with all the conveniences of a first-class hotel, and is kept open during the whole year.

CATSKILL MOUNTAIN HOUSE.—For miles up and down the river, and from almost any point in the six counties we have mentioned as under the jurisdiction of the Catskills, we can see the "Mountain House," *three thousand feet above the river*, like a bit of snow left on the mountains. This hotel is only ten or eleven miles from the landing, and the ride from the village is pleasant and romantic. This hotel has been for years the favorite summer resort on the river, and its popularity is continually on the increase. No European traveler ever thinks of leaving it unvisited. The Catskills and Niagara Falls are two points *known everywhere.*

These mountains are, indeed, the glory of the Hudson, and have been poetically termed, "the ever-changing legendary Kaatsbergs." They were called by the Indians the Onti-o-ras, or Mountains of the Sky, as they sometimes seem like clouds along the horizon. This range of mountains was supposed by the Indians to have been originally a monster who devoured all the children of the Red Men, and that the Great Spirit touched him when he was going down to the salt lake to bathe, and here he remains. "Two little lakes upon the summit were regarded as the eyes of the monster, and these are open all the summer; but in the winter they are covered with a thick crust or heavy film; but whether sleeping or waking, tears always trickle down his cheeks. Here, according to Indian belief, was kept the great treasury of storm and sunshine, presided over by an old squaw spirit who dwelt on the highest peak of the mountains. She kept day and night shut up in her wigwam, letting out only one at a time. She manufactured new moons every month, cutting up the old ones into stars, and, like the old Æolus of mythology, shut the winds up in the caverns of the hills." A morning view from this cliff will be remembered a lifetime; at least we remember, as if it were yesterday, a July morning three years ago. We rose at 3.30, at least an hour before

"Night murmured to the morning,—
Lie still, oh! love, lie still."

Patiently we waited the sun's advent, and as the rosy dawn announced the morning coming with "looks all vernal and with cheeks all bloom," the *windows* of the Mountain House, one after another, began to reveal undreamed visions of loveliness, and it were really difficult to tell which had the deeper interest, the sun's rising in the east, or the daughters in the west. The rosy clouds of the one, the tender blushes of the other; the opening eyelids of the morning, or the opening eyelids of innocence; the bright ambrosial locks hanging far and wide along the deep blue chiseled mountain side, or the *uncombed* ripples which, like mountain streams receiving additions from other sources, would probably become beautiful waterfalls. In four minutes more by solar time, and the sun would sprinkle the golden dust of light over the valley of the Hudson. The East was all aglow, and, *as we stood musing the fire burned*, yes, brighter and brighter, as if the distant hills were an altar, and a sacrifice was being offered up to the God of Day. It truly reminded one of an Oriental dry-goods store, with costly goods in the show-windows running opposition to the muslin and dimity-filled window-cases in the west.

Cities and villages below us sprang into being, and misty shapes rose from the valley, as if Day had rolled back the stone from the Sepulcher of Night, and it was rising transfigured to Heaven. Adown and up the river for the distance of sixty miles, sloops and schooners drifted lazily along, while below us the little

"ferry-boats plied
Like slow shuttles through the sunny warp
Of threaded silver from a thousand brooks."

Truly the Catskills were a fitting place for the artist Cole to gather inspiration to complete that beautiful series of paintings, "The Voyage

of Life," for no finer mountains in all the world overlook a finer river. Irving, in writing of his first voyage up the Hudson, "in the good old times before steamboats and railroads had annihilated time and space, and driven all poetry and romance out of travel," says: "But of all the scenery of the Hudson the Kaatskill Mountains had the most witching effect on my boyish imagination. Never shall I forget the effect upon me of the first view of them, predominating over a wide extent of country,—part wild, woody, and rugged, part softened away into all the graces of cultivation. As we slowly floated along I lay on the deck and watched them through a long summer's day; undergoing a thousand mutations under the magical effects of atmosphere; sometimes seeming to approach; at other times to recede; now almost melting into hazy distance, now burnished by the setting sun, until in the evening they printed themselves against the glowing sky in the deep purple of an Italian landscape." On preceeding page we presented a cut of the Mountain House, furnished by Mr. C. L. Beach, proprietor. This favorite summer resort, so justly celebrated for its grand scenery and healthful atmosphere, will be open from June 1st to October 1st. Ready access may be had at all times by Mr. Beach's stages connecting at the village of Catskill with the Hudson River steamboats and the trains on the Hudson River Railroad. Two miles from the hotel are the Kaaterskill Falls. The waters fall perpendicularly 175 feet, and afterward 85 feet more. A sort of amphitheater behind the cascade is the scene of one of Bryant's finest poems:—

"From greens and shades where the Catterskill leaps
From cliffs where the wood flowers cling;"

and we recall the lines which express so beautifully the well-nigh fatal dream:—

"Of that dreaming one
By the base of that icy steep
When over his stiffening limbs begun
The deadly slumbers of frost to creep.
    *   *   *
There pass the chasers of seal and whale,
With their weapons quaint and grim,
And bands of warriors in glittering mail,
And herdsmen and hunters huge of limb,
There are naked arms with bow and spear
And furry gauntlets the carbine roar.

About half-way up the mountain is the place said to be the dreamland of Rip Van Winkle—the greatest character of American Mythology, more real than the heroes of Homer or the massive gods of Olympus. And our age has reason to congratulate itself on the *possession* of Joseph Jefferson and John Rogers, who on the stage and in the studio have illustrated to the life this master-piece of Irving.

The cut here given repesents Rip Van Winkle at home, the favorite

of the village children. You will remember Irving says, "the children of the village would shout with joy whenever he approached, he assisted at their sports, made them playthings, taught them to fly kites and shoot marbles, and told them long stories of ghosts, witches and Indians. Whenever he went dodging about the village he was surrounded by a troop of them hanging on his skirts, clambering on his back and playing a thousand tricks on him with impunity." Two others complete the group, Rip Van Winkle on the mountains, and Rip Van Winkle returned. As will be seen above, the figure of Rip was modelled from Mr. Jefferson, who sat for his likeness. And as we turn away from the Catskills, with their visions of beauty and reality of fiction, we can only say, don't fail to hear the great actor when opportunity occurs, don't fail to read again the story of Irving, and don't fail to have the finest group of statuary in the world,—price twelve dollars each.

These, with the courtship of Ichabod and Katrina, give an artistic delineation of the comic-tragedy and the tragic-comedy of the Hudson. A stamp enclosed to John Rogers, 212 Fifth Avenue, will procure a fine illustrated catalogue and price-list.

Catskill was for many years the home of Cole, the artist; and the new residence of Church will be seen almost opposite, on the east bank.

At Wanton Island, near Catskill, it is said the last Indian battle was fought upon the river, between the Mohawks and the Mohegans.

HUDSON, six miles north of Catskill, was founded in the year 1784, by thirty persons from Providence, R. I. It is a city of ten thousand inhabitants, and has the finest court-house and grounds on the river. We believe it is also the only city that has a fine promenade park overlooking the Hudson. It has long enjoyed the reputation of hospitality, and strangers always receive a kindly welcome. This is the western terminus of the Hudson and Boston Railroad, one of the oldest railroads in the country. At Chatham Village it connects with the Boston and Albany, the Harlem, and the Harlem Extension.

LEBANON SPRINGS.—The day-line of steamers makes one of the finest routes to the popular summer resort of Lebanon Springs, and one of the pleasantest round trips that can be made from New York, to wit: Take the "Vibbard" or "Daniel Drew" to Hudson, 115 miles; cars to Chatham, 20 miles; connecting with Harlem Extension Railroad for Lebanon Springs, 15 miles. In this way we enjoy a pleasant sail up the river, and arrive at the Springs in the afternoon. Stay at Columbia Hall as long as you can; visit the Shakers; and then return to New York via Harlem Railroad, visiting Bash-Bish Falls (six miles from Hillsdale, one mile from Copake); also Stone Church at Dover Plains, and Lake Mahopac. The trip can be easily made in three or four days.

Columbia Hall, **Daniel Gale** Proprietor, has a charming location, and looks down from its hillside upon that beautiful valley which reminded Henry Vincent of the scenery of Llangollen, in Wales.

ATHENS, directly opposite Hudson, is suggestive of at least one thing, that we have names on the Hudson of all *complexions*—Troy, Athens, Tivoli, and Carthage, "mixed up" with English, Dutch, and Indian names of every dialect. An old Mohegan village, known as Potick, was located west of Athens.

After leaving Hudson we pass Stockport on the east side, and Coxsackie on the west (name derived from an Indian word signifying cut banks; others say Cooks-ockay, owl-hooting; and others from Kaak-aki, a *place of geese*).

STUYVESANT, ten miles north of Hudson, on the east bank, was once known as Kinderhook Point, or Landing, and took its name from an old Swedish family with numerous progeny, that once lived on a point half a mile above the landing—Kinder-hook signifying Children's Corner, or Point. The village of Kinderhook is the finest in Columbia County, five miles from the landing. *Lindenwold*, the home of Martin Van Buren, is about two miles from the village. Columbia is one of the few counties in our republic that can boast a President of the United States.

The villages of New Baltimore and Coeymans are on the west bank. Schodack Landing and Castleton on the east. In digging for the foundation of a house at Coeyman's, in the winter of 1872, it is said that ruins of the old castle were discovered, where Anthony Van Corlear blew his trumpet in vain, and carried back certain signs to the good people of New Amsterdam, strange to behold (see Irving's Knickerbocker).

SCHODACK.—The township of Schodack is one of the oldest and pleasantest in the County of Rensselaer, and was the head-centre or capital of the Mohegan tribe. It has its origin in the word *Scholi*, signifying fire; and *ack*, place; or the place of the ever-burning council-fire of the Mohegan tribe. Here King Acpgin, the 8th of April, 1680, sold to Van Rensselaer "all that tract of country on the west side of the Hudson, extending from Beeren Island up to Smack's Island, and in breadth two day's journey."

THE MOHEGAN TRIBE originally occupied all the east bank of the Hudson north of Roeliffe Jansen's Kill, near Germantown, to the head waters of the Hudson; and, on the west bank, from Cohoes to Catskill. The town of Schodack was central, and a signal displayed from the hills near Castleton could be seen for thirty miles in every direction. After the Mohegans left the Hudson, they went to Westenhook, or Housatonic, to the hills south of Stockbridge; and then, on invitation of the Oneidas, removed to Oneida County, 1785, where they lived until 1821, when, with other Indians of New York, they purchased a tract of land near Fox River, Minnesota.

The Mourder's Kill flows into the Hudson just above Castleton. The Norman's Kill flows into the Hudson a few miles above, on the west side. It was called by the Indians the Tawasentha, or "place of many dead." We are now in sight of Albany, and our summer day is drawing to a close.

ALBANY is a city of about eighty thousand inhabitants, and one of the most flourishing in the State. Its prosperity is due to, at least, three causes. First, the capital was removed from New York to Albany in 1798. Then followed two great enterprises, ridiculed at the time by every one as the *Fulton Folly* and *Clinton's Ditch;* in other words, steam navigation, 1807, and the Erie Canal, 1825. Tourists and travelers will find interest in visiting the old and new Capitol, the State Hall, the City Hall, and the Dudley Observatory, to the north of the city; and, during their stay, they will find the best care and attention at the "Delavan House." This hotel is complete in all its appointments, and is known everywhere as one of the best in the State.

The Albany Cathedral is also a grand structure, and will well repay a visit. The iron fence about it was made at the Albany Iron and Machine Works (H. C. Haskell, Proprietor), and is probably the finest work of its kind in the United States. The railing, also, on the new bridge across the Hudson at Albany, is of their manufacture, to which we call the respectful attention of all who have a taste for art and beauty, in this "age of iron." During the past winter he completed one of his fine engines for the Government Printing House in Washington, and it is pronounced the most effective in our country. He has recently erected a new building near the steamboat landing and the depot of the Albany and Susquehanna Railroad, four stories high, fifty feet by sixty, which increases his facilities for doing with promptness and despatch his continually increasing business.

The site of Albany was called by the Indians Shaunaugh-ta-da, or the Pine Plains, a name which we still see in Schenectada. From an old book in the State Library, we condense the following description,

DELAVAN HOUSE.

Charles E. Leland & Co., Proprietors.

presenting quite a contrast to its modern business activity. "Albany lay stretched along the banks of the Hudson, on one very wide and long street, parallel to the Hudson. The space between the street and the river-bank was occupied by gardens. A small but steep hill rose above the centre of the town, on which stood a fort. The wide street leading to the fort (now State Street) had a Market Place, Guard-House, Town Hall, and an English and Dutch Church, in the centre."

It is also said that Albany existed one hundred years without a lawyer, even as Rome five hundred without a physician. Its name, as we said before, was given in honor of the Duke of Albany, although it is still claimed by some of the oldest inhabitants, that, in the golden age of those far-off times, when the good old burghers used to ask for the welfare of their neighbors, the answer was always "All bonnie," and hence the name of the hill-crowned city.

And now, while waiting to "throw out the plank," which puts a period to our Hudson River Division, we feel like congratulating ourselves that the various goblins which once infested the river have become civilized, that the winds and tides have been conquered, and that the nine-day voyage of Hendrich Hudson and the "Half Moon" has been reduced to the *nine-hour system* of the "Vibbard" and the "Drew."

Those who have traveled over Europe will certainly appreciate the quiet luxury of an American steamer; and this first introduction to American scenery will always charm the tourist from other lands. Three years ago it was my privilege to visit some of the rivers and lakes of the old world, well known in song and story, but I imagine that no single day's journey in any land or on any stream can present such variety, interest, and beauty, as the trip of one hundred and forty-four miles from New York to Albany. The Hudson is indeed a goodly volume, with its broad covers of green *lying open* on either side; and it might in truth be called a *condensed* history, for there is no place in our country where poetry and romance are so strangely blended with the heroic and the historic,—no river where the waves of different civilizations have left so many waifs upon the banks. It is classic ground, from the "wilderness to the sea," and will always be

THE POETS' CORNER OF OUR COUNTRY;

the home of Irving, Willis, and Morris,—of Fulton, Morse, and Field,—of Cole, Audubon, and Church,—and scores besides, whose names are **Household Words.**

ONE of the interesting features of Albany is the celebrated Clothing House of Davis & Co. No one should leave the city without paying it

a visit. If tourists want anything in their line, they will be honorably dealt by. We can recommend the Establishment in every particular.

DELAWARE AND HUDSON CANAL COMPANY.

ALBANY AND SUSQUEHANNA DEPARTMENT.—There are few railroads in our country that possess for so many miles such variety and interest as the Albany and Susquehanna. All the way from Albany to Binghamton the hills and valleys, the streams, rivulets, and rivers form a succession of beautiful landscapes, framed in the moving panorama of a car window. The railroad follows the valleys of three streams—the Schoharie, the Cobleskill, and the Susquehanna.

Leaving Albany we pass through the little villages and stations of Adamsville, Slingerlands, New Scotland, Guilderland, Knowersville, Dunnesburgh, Quaker Street, Esperance, and come to Central Bridge, thirty-six miles from Albany, the junction with the branch road for Schoharie Court-House and Middleburgh. Schoharie village, the county seat, is situated on Schoharie Flats. First settlement made in 1711. Population about fifteen hundred. The old stone church, erected in 1772, is now used as an arsenal. Three miles from Central Bridge, or thirty-nine miles from Albany, is the celebrated

HOWE'S CAVE, discovered on the 22d May, 1842, by Lester Howe. In interest and extent it is second only to the great Mammoth Cave of Kentucky, and presents, in truth, a new world of beauty, with arches and walls reaching away for miles, of which perhaps the half is only discovered. Among the prominent points of interest in the cave are the following, as named by Mr. Howe:—

"Reception, or Lecture Room," "Washington Hall," "Bridal Chamber," (temperature 48 deg. Fah.), where many have been nuptually tied, including the two daughters of the discoverer; "The Chapel," some forty feet high; "Harlequin Tunnel," "Cataract Hall," "Ghost Room, or Haunted Castle," "Music Hall," "Stygian, or Crystal Lake." At the foot of the lake there are several gas-burners, giving the visitor a beautiful view of that portion of the cave and lake, and the side grotto near by. From thence visitors proceed by boats across the lake to "Plymouth Rock," and from thence continue the journey to the "Devil's Gateway," "The Museum," "Geological Rooms," "Uncle Tom's Cabin," "Giants' Study," "Pirates' Cave," "Rocky Mountains," "Valley of Jehosophat," "Winding Way," and "Rotunda." There are the usual formations, known as "Stalagmites" and "Stalactites," many of them singular in form and variety. In Washington Hall are two, named "Lady Washington's Hood" and "Washington's Epaulet;" and beyond these are "The Harp," and numberless others. At the head and foot of the lake there are two large stalagmites, the former large enough to fill the entire body of the cave, which has made it necessary to excavate an artificial passage around it. These are among the most wonderful formations in the cave, and of particular interest to the geological and scientific student.

We are only able to mark out the route in this hasty manner. To speak of all the objects of interest would draw us aside from the purpose of a general guide. The "Cave House" is a fine hotel, recently erected at the mouth of the cave, and the wants of the tourist and explorer will be carefully attended to. Every one should visit Howe's Cave, and see these real Arabian Night beauties, so near the capital of the Empire State.

The next station is Cobleskill, forty-five miles from Albany. This rich and fertile valley was called by the Indians Ots-ga-ra-ga. The village is thriving and flourishing. Smith's "National Hotel" is one of the best on the route, and decidedly the best in the place. This is also the junction of the Cherry Valley Branch, which passes through Hyndsville, Seward, and Sharon Springs.

SHARON SPRINGS is one of the oldest and most satisfactory summer resorts. The village is splendidly located—as we said years ago, on our first visit—*in a valley on a hill*. The streets are well shaded. There are nine large hotels, always full. One of the pleasantest of these—in location and every point of comfort—is the "Union," a cut of which is here given. The cool and shaded verandahs, the large and well-furnished rooms, and every luxury in its season, combine to make it a pleasant place to spend a summer season.

The picturesque scenery of Sharon and environs, and the beautiful park promenades and drives, have made this summer resort one of the most frequented in the United States. The Sulphur, Magnesia, and Chalybeate Springs have a fine reputation for the cure of cutaneous diseases. Since the completion of the Branch Railroad from Cobleskill it is very easy of access,—only two hours from Albany *via* the pleasant drawing-room coaches of the Albany and Susquehanna Department.

UNION HOUSE, SHARON SPRINGS, N. Y.
CHARLES SCHWARZ, Proprietor.

CHERRY VALLEY.—The next station to Sharon is Cherry Valley, a pleasant town in the northeast corner of Otsego County; and from this point a stage-line connects with Richfield Springs, and its long-established and popular hotel, the "American House." Returning to Cobleskill we pursue our route westward on the main line of the Albany and Susquehanna; and we pass through Richmondville, lying in a valley on our left; then East Worcester, Worcester, Schenevus, and Maryland, to the junction of the Cooperstown and Susquehanna Valley Railroad for Portlandsville, Milford, Clinton, Phœnix, and

COOPERSTOWN, one of the pleasantest villages in New York, and one of the classic points of our country. It is situated on the shore of Otsego, a beautiful lake, worthy of being the fountain-head of the bright flowing Susquehanna. Every one who has read "The Deerslayer" or "The Pioneer" knows something of its beauty. The name Otsego signifies "friendly greeting," from the fact that a small rock near the shore was a rendezvous where the tribes were wont to assemble; and its name is still significant to the tourist and traveler, for the "Cooper House" is indeed a place of "friendly greeting," and has for its motto the old Scotch proverb, "Welcome the coming, and speed the

COOPER HOUSE, COOPERSTOWN, N. Y.
(Foot of Otsego Lake.)
COLEMAN & MAXWELL, Proprietors.

parting." In the hands of its present popular proprietors—William B. Coleman, of the "New York Hotel," and Albert Maxwell, late superintendent of the "Union Club,"—it has won the first position as a place of summer resort. The hotel is, in every particular, one of the finest and best-furnished in the United States. It stands on the highest ground in the village—80 feet above the lake, 1200 feet above the sea—and is surrounded by a fine park of over seven acres, handsomely planted with shade-trees; and with croquet, ball, and archery grounds within the inclosure. The internal arrangements of the house are complete with all the modern improvements, including bells, gas in every room, hot and cold baths, &c.

There are also desirable cottages, containing six, twelve, and twenty-two rooms each.

The surroundings of Cooperstown are delightful in every particular, and there are fine drives in every direction. Mount Vision, a little to the north, overlooks the village; and still further to the north is Prospect Cliff. Otsego Lake, like Lake Mahopac, is literally surrounded with beauty; and, like Irvington or Tarrytown, Cooperstown is one of the literary Meccas of our country. It is the place to read the works of Cooper; for, in reading them, we are here surrounded by the same inspiration which produced them. In his "Deerslayer" we have the finest description of the lake and surrounding hills. "On a level with the point lay a broad sheet of water, so placid and limpid that it resembled a *bed of the pure mountain atmosphere* compressed into a setting of hills and woods. At its northern or nearest end it was bounded by an isolated mountain; lower land falling off east and west, gracefully relieving the sweep of the outline; still the character of the country was mountainous; high hills or low mountains rising abruptly from the water on quite nine-tenths of its circuit. But the most striking peculiarity of the scene were its solemn solitude and sweet repose. On all sides, wherever the eye turned, nothing met it but the mirror-like surface of the lake, the placid view of heaven, and the dense setting of woods. So rich and fleecy were the outlines of the forest, that the whole visible earth, from the rounded mountain-top to the water's edge presented one unvaried hue of unbroken verdure." The same points still exist which "Leather Stocking" then saw. There is the same beauty of verdure along the hills, and the sun still glints as brightly as then the ripples of the clear water. There are some things that are constant even upon earth, and surely the unchanging stars should have a changeless mirror! Cooper himself says in the preface, "Even the points exist, a little altered by civilization, but so nearly answering to the description as to be easily recognized by all who are familiar with the scenery of this particular region."

The Cemetery, we venture to say, has a finer location than any in the State; and Natty Bumppo looks down from his marble shaft upon the bright "Glimmerglass" which recalls his memory. The new steamboat, also named after the great hunter, will run three times a day during the season, touching at Three-Mile Point, Five-Mile Point, and Springfield Landing, connecting with a new line of stages at the head of the lake for Richfield Springs. There will also be frequent pleasure-trips around the lake.

Cooperstown is within four hours from Albany or Binghamton by rail, and there is communication twice each way daily. Omnibuses will run regularly from the "Cooper House," to and from the steamer and favorite prospects. In the central part of the village is a pleasant hotel styled the "Central House," W. C. Keyes & Son, proprietors. It is kept open summer and winter, and justly deserves the fine reputation it has obtained among persons traveling, either on business or pleasure. In addition to the natural beauty of this county seat of Otsego, we must not overlook the following enterprise of the citizens. The business men of Cooperstown, being desirous to attract manufactories or any producing enterprises which will add to its population and trade, offer through a committee of the "Improvement Society," to *give* a suitable lot or building site to any responsible parties who will conduct such business there. Further aid in the way of capital, residences, &c., would also be given where the undertaking justified or required it. Desirable homestead lots can also be obtained on or near the lake or river at very low prices.

The last census returns show Cooperstown to be one of the most healthful localities in the State, as well as being highly favored in its public school, library, and reading-room, and other educational facilities.

There are many elegant residences in the village. The house and grounds of Edward Clark are noted throughout the State. For fuller particulars in reference to the historic interest and living poetry of Cooperstown we call your attention to a descriptive essay by Barry Gray, entitled "The home of Cooper, and the haunts of Leather-stocking;" and while you are waiting to take a pleasant lake trip to another watering-place near at hand, we will quote a sentence from

Mr. Seward's address at Cherry Valley, July 4th, 1840, which each person may appropriately repeat: "I have desired to see for myself the valleys of Otsego, through which the Susquehanna extends his arms and entwines his fingers with the tributaries of the Mohawk, as if to divert that gentle river from its allegiance to the Hudson."

RICHFIELD SPRINGS.—Of all routes to this popular summer resort, there is none so picturesque and pleasant as this we have indicated, *via* Cooperstown and Otsego Lake. Of course, persons in a hurry will take a drawing-room coach at the New York Grand Central Depot, and in eight hours, without change of cars, be set down at the doors of the pleasant and hospitable "American." The village is noted everywhere as one of the healthiest in the State; and its fine springs have been to many true "fountains of youth." The "American Hotel" is one of the oldest established resorts in the country, and its popularity has ever been on the increase. It has a fine location fronting the pavilion and pleasant grounds of the Richfield Sulphur Springs. This new line across the lake will make a pleasant interchange between the guests of Richfield and Cooperstown, and will be very popular. The drive across is also very fine, either along the shore of Schuyler Lake or Otsego. There is a hill about two miles from Richfield, from which one will see seven lakes, all lying within a radius of ten miles.

Returning now to the main line of the Albany and Susquehanna Railroad, we can pursue our western journey through Collier's and Emmons', to Oneonta, one of the most stirring villages on the route. The next station is Otego. From this point stages connect with the pleasant village of Franklin, well known through its prosperous seminary and educational enterprise. Passing through Wells' Bridge, Unadilla, Sidney (with its branch road to Delhi), Afton, and Harpersville, we come to the Tunnel, 127 miles from New York. Then passing through Osborn Hollow and Port Crane, we come to Binghamton, and complete the equilateral triangle—New York, Albany, and Binghamton. It is a flourishing city of 16,000 inhabitants, and has complete railway connections with the Erie, the Delaware Lackawana and Western, and Syracuse and Binghamton railways. The best hotel is the "Spaulding House," only a short distance from the depot.

Mrs. H. H. CARY.   Mrs. WM. P. JOHNSON.   G. W. TUNNICLIFF.

American Hotel,

1873—RICHFIELD SPRINGS—1873
OTSEGO COUNTY, N. Y.

WM. P. JOHNSON & CO., PROPRIETORS.

The reputation of the "AMERICAN" is so well established as a first-class Summer Hotel—the favorite resort of families seeking a pleasant home during the warm weather—that it needs no introduction to the public. It is situated directly opposite the celebrated Richfield Sulphur Springs, and has recently been enlarged by the erection of a new wing, which adds 100 rooms to its former accommodations; the grand parlor has been enlarged; Gas has been introduced through the entire House, and general improvements made throughout; much new Furniture has been added. There is a fine Sulphur Spring, recently discovered and tubed, in the basement of the Hotel. It is impossible to estimate too highly the great Medicinal value of these Waters for all Cutaneous Diseases, Rheumatism, Gout, &c., as thousands will testify who have been cured by their use.

Visitors can come all the way from New York by Railroad, as the road to Richfield Springs, connected with the New York Central R. R., at Utica, is now open. Drawing Room Cars will be run direct from New York City to Richfield Springs during the coming season. Visitors from Philadelphia can reach Richfield Springs via Delaware, Lackawanna and Western R. R. Those coming to the Springs via Susquehanna and Cooperstown Railroads, will find an excellent line of stages leaving twice a day, running between Cooperstown and Richfield Springs, a distance of 14 miles. Baggage checked through, over either route, from New York or Philadelphia to Richfield Springs.

TERMS OF BOARD.

Per Day, - - - - - $4	Per Week, 2 weeks, - -	$20 to $23
Per Week, 1 week, - - - 21 to $25	Per Week, 4 weeks or longer, -	18 to 20

According to Location and Size of Rooms.

A Double Room occupied by one person, price and a half.
Children and Servants at the Children's table, $10 per week.

Drawing Room Cars 8½ hours from New York without Change.

The American House has this season been thoroughly renovated in the culinary department, and the new and commodious sewers lately built in the village renders the drainage from this House thorough and complete.

NIAGARA FALLS, AND THE NEW YORK CENTRAL RAILROAD.

At the unveiling of Shakespeare's monument in Central Park, William Cullen Bryant said, *What Niagara is to other waterfalls Shakespeare is to other poets.* In the converse of this sentence we have a happy expression of Niagara's greatness and grandeur, for it is in truth the crowning glory of our continent.

The route from Albany is via "The New York Central," one of the best-appointed railroads in our country; furnished with Wagner's elegant drawing-room cars and Pullman coaches. There are five through trains from New York to Niagara Falls; and this route combines speed with the greatest comfort. In fact, our times have outgrown the inconveniences of travel. The dream of Arabian fancy is realized. These sumptuous saloons remind one of the "enchanted carpet" which wafted the traveler from place to place.

Leaving the domes of the river-crowned capital behind us, we pass through Schenectady, Fonda, Palatine Bridge, Fort Plain, and places of minor interest, and come to Little Falls, the head centre of Herkimer cheese. Here the gentle Mohawk of the poet rushes through a rock channel of remarkable formation, and we come to the conclusion that the writer of

"How sweet is the vale where the Mohawk gently glides"

was not a native of Herkimer. We get, from the car window, quite a good view of the river and its rocky channel. A few miles further bring us to

UTICA—the first express station—ninety-five miles from Albany. This, in continental days, was the site of old Fort Schuyler, and now one of the most flourishing towns in Central New York. Passengers for Trenton Falls here take the Utica and Black River Railroad to Trenton,—a passage of scenery not only wild and romantic, but also rendered poetic by the pen of N. P. Willis. These falls—six in number—are well worth a visit.

Passengers for Richfield Springs will be carried by drawing-room cars without change, and will be safely set down at the American Hotel,—about three hours' run from Albany. The attractions in and about Utica will well repay a few days' visit. The pleasantest hotel in the city is the "Butterfield House," a few blocks removed from the noise and turmoil of the depot. A cut of this hotel is here given. It is complete in every particular, and situated in the central and business

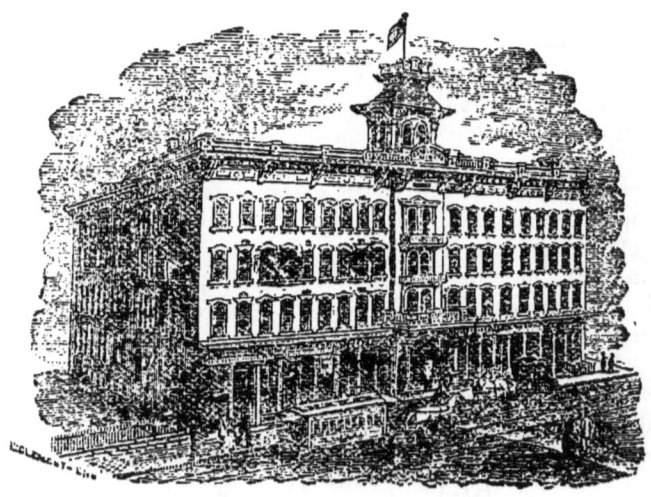

THE BUTTERFIELD HOUSE, UTICA, N. Y.

Oscar R. Stone & Co., Proprietors.

part of the city. Free omnibuses to and from the cars. We also imagine there is no city which even passing strangers hold in better remembrance, as this furnishes the best restaurant on the line of the Central Railroad, and Mr. D. M. Johnson's lunch-boxes, furnished with goodly provisions—price $1.00—are known by every one the whole length of the line.

Passing through Rome, where persons connect with the "Rome, Watertown, and Ogdensburgh" line for the Thousand Islands, the St. Lawrence Rapids, and Montreal, our next city of importance is

SYRACUSE, 148 miles from Albany, one of the most flourishing and enterprising towns of Central New York, and almost as well salted as old Sodom and Gomorrah, the cities of the plain. Here are railroad connections for Binghamton and Oswego; and here, also, the Old and New Central diverges, meeting again at

ROCHESTER, 229 miles from Albany, the finest city of Western New York, and in some particulars the finest in the State. It is situated on the Genesee River, which we cross as we come into the city; and we get a view, on our right, of the falls where Sam Patch made the last *extempore* effort of his life. The Genesee has fine water-power, and the falls also furnished successful inspiration to one of Daniel Webster's finest efforts. The best hotel is the "Osborn House," centrally located. Passing through Brockport, Albion, Medina, and Lockport, we come to

SUSPENSION BRIDGE, 304 miles from Albany, the first great enterprise of the New World; for, without being personal, there was certainly "a great gulf fixed" between the United States and Canada, until one day a little kite-string drew a wire across the chasm, and the wire grew and multiplied until the spider-like art hung a thousand tons in equipoise. Two miles now bring us to

NIAGARA FALLS, and, making our way through throngs of porters and carriages, whose clamor drowns even the roar of the waters, we soon find ourselves safely and quietly located in the pleasant rooms of the "International,"—appropriately named, for scenery like Niagara, even if Canada were a part of our country, could never belong to one nation or people. It is *International.* It belongs to the world. This hotel, under the supervision of James T. Fulton, owner and proprietor, has won a wide reputation for civility and attention to travelers. It is the largest and most pleasantly situated at Niagara, having ample accommodation for over six hundred guests. During the past winter it has been thoroughly refitted, and an elegant addition, comprising suites of rooms, and three magnificent public parlors, extending one hundred feet into the rapids, has been made, and, being nearer the Falls than any other hotel, it is now unsurpassed for comfort, location, and scenery. Railroad, steamboat, and telegraph offices in the building. Omnibuses and porters at all trains. A fine cut of the hotel is here given, furnished by the courtesy of Mr. Henry Morford, whose fine handbooks on American and European travel are favorably known on either side of the Atlantic.

INTERNATIONAL HOTEL, NIAGARA FALLS, N. Y.

JAMES T. FULTON, Proprietor.

And now, being comfortably located, we will proceed to take a look at the "scenery." A few steps bring us to the American Falls (900 feet across, and 164 feet high). We have all seen pictures of these falls, from Church's masterpiece to the hastily engraved cut of a Guide-Book; we all have an idea how the falls *look;* but they never speak to us until we have looked over that deep abyss and up the stream which ever rushes on like an army to battle, and miles down the crowded channel where the black waters have worn their passage, through the silent, unknown centuries. Remember what they say to you, oh, hearer! and as you look upon them the first time uncover your head a single moment. The *language* is addressed to your soul. One-eighth of a mile below these falls is the new Suspension Bridge, the longest in the world—1800 feet in length, the towers 100 feet high, and cables 1800 feet long. This carriage and foot-way was long needed, and now not only presents a fine view of the Falls from every stand-point, but affords the most convenient route to the views on the Canada side. It was opened to the public January 4th, 1869. Goat Island, the natural Central Park of the Falls, is connected with the American side by a bridge. The area of the island is about sixty acres. In our hasty sketch we will, however, only name the places to be visited, leaving the description to the local guide books. The Cave of the Winds, with its magnificent curtain of changing beauty,. the Rainbow, the Whirlpool Rapids, reached by the Double Elevator. Terrapin Bridge and Prospect Tower, overlooking Horse Shoe Falls (about 1900 feet wide and 158 feet high). On the Canada side the principal points of interest are Table Rock and the broad Causeway, where one can feel all the glory of Niagara, and where Mrs. Sigourney wrote those expressive lines—

" God has set
His rainbow on thy forehead, and the clouds
Mantled around thy feet."

Burning Spring is about a mile above Table Rock, near the river edge. Not far from this the battle of Chippewa was fought, July 5, 1814. And also, a mile and a half from the falls, is the battle ground of Lundy's Lane. The Suspension Bridge, two miles below, is a triumph in art; the Whirlpool is about a mile below this bridge. Many writers have attempted to describe Niagara, but in every description there is something lacking. We can give its dimensions, its height and breadth, and point out the places to be seen; but there is a *Unity* about Niagara which can only be felt. It makes one wish that David could have seen it, and added a new chapter to the Psalms. It surely would not have been out of place in the chapter following "The heavens declare the glory of God, the firmament showeth His handiwork." In happy reminiscence the great English novelist has perhaps written its best description: "I think in every quiet season, now, still do these waters roll, and leap, and roar, and tumble, all day long. Still are the rainbows spanning them, a hundred feet below. Still, when the sun is on them, do they shine and glow like molten gold. Still, when the day is gloomy, do they fall like snow, or seem to crumble away like the front of a great chalk cliff, or roll down the rock like dense white smoke. But always does the mighty stream appear to die as it comes down, and always from the unfathomable grave arises that tremendous ghost of spray and mist which is never laid, which has haunted the place with the same dread solemnity since darkness brooded on the deep, and that first flood before the deluge—Light—came rushing on Creation at the word of God."

From Niagara tourists may make the round trip to Montreal, Lake Champlain, Lake George, and Saratoga, or the still longer round trip to Montreal, the Green and White Mountains, and so to New York, via Portland and Boston. Tourists taking either of these trips have *two routes* to Montreal—one via the Grand Trunk Railroad, the other via boat down the lake and St. Lawrence. The rapids and islands are interesting features of the route, and we refer to them again in our article on "Montreal and the Thousand Islands."

TOURISTS WILL FIND

The best Summer and Winter Stereoscopic Views of

N I A G A R A   F A L L S,

AT

MR. GEO. BARKER'S,

Almost opposite the International Hotel.

FIFTEEN HUNDRED DISTINCT VIEWS.

Also, Indian Work and Curiosities.

FROM NIAGARA FALLS TO PHILADELPHIA, BALTIMORE,
AND WASHINGTON,
VIA
ROCHESTER, CANANDAIGUA, PENN-YAN, WATKINS' GLEN,
ELMIRA, WILLIAMSPORT, AND HARRISBURGH.

This route—from Niagara to Philadelphia and Washington—presents some of the finest scenery of New York and Pennsylvania; and makes

SENECA LAKE.

one of the best round trips to be taken in connection with the day-line of the Hudson and the route we have just indicated to Niagara. Tourists may also reverse the order, going direct from Philadelphia to Niagara and Watkins' Glen, and then to Albany and down the Hudson to New York.

These beautiful glens—Watkins and Glenola, near the shores of Seneca Lake—have been poetically styled "a secluded mystery of beauties which the elements have been for ages carving and decorating." No person, in fact, can be said to *do* New York State thoroughly without paying them a visit. During the last few years there have been many descriptive articles giving an idea of their general character; but, like all descriptions, they fall short in the expression. One of the best of these—at least in point of brevity—was published in *Scribner's*, 1872; and we subjoin the following description of

THE GLEN, or cabinet edition of a Colorado canyon: "Here we see

THE GLEN MOUNTAIN HOUSE.

a placid pool, there a thundering waterfall, beyond a ribbon of foam, where the stream tears through a crooked rift in the rocks; then a series of rippling cascades, followed by long reaches of still water, so clear and glassy that one seems to look through the slaty bottom into an under world of fantastic forms—an inverted spiritual counterpart of the wonderful region round and above. Now the stream overspreads a broad channel, as level as a pavement; now it rushes through a narrow sluice-way, and again sleeps in a chain of oval pools, the footprints of waterfalls long since receded." These various points are so rapidly and poetically referred to in the above quotation that it reminds one of the musical poem often read by elocutionists, "The way the water comes down at Ladore."

HECTOR FALLS.

The double fall of Hector, in the neighborhood, is well worthy of a summer day's excursion, "where a stream much larger than any of the Glen streams, leaps into the lake over a quick succession of bold cliffs, falling two hundred feet or more in as many yards."

From Watkins' Glen our route will take us via Elmira to Minequa, with its noted Springs; and Williamsport, with its fine hotel,—the "Herdic House."

At Northumberland, forty miles south of Williamsport, the north and west branches of the Susquehanna meet. The north branch, you will remember, takes its rise in Otsego Lake, at Cooperstown (referred to in our article on the route to Cooperstown, Sharon and Richfield Springs), and is famous in poetry and history for the cruel tragedy of Wyoming, and the stirring scenes on its banks. You will also remember Campbell's beautiful line—

"On Susquehanna's side, fair Wyoming."

And now we pass the marriage of two poetic streams, where the "blue Juniata" is willing to change her name, and, in maiden modesty, *give all herself* to her liquid Romeo. Then, thirty-seven miles to Lancaster, where Robert Fulton, when a boy, made his first paddle-wheels; and Thaddeus Stevens and Buchanan lived. Then sixty miles bring us to Bryn Mawr, a pleasant village in the suburbs of Philadelphia, with station and railway appointments suggesting an English landscape, and so to Philadelphia, with its pleasant streets, "that re-echo the names of the trees of the forest."

It is probably the most quiet and orderly city in the world for its size. Although it has a population of about 700,000, and possesses stirring business activity and enterprise, still the quiet genius of its great founder seems to reign supreme. The most pleasant, quiet, and convenient hotel is the "Colonnade House," John Crump, Proprietor, a cut of which is given on the opposite page. The tourist can spend a number of days in Philadelphia with profit; and, in addition to its commercial activity, it has a decent and respectful reverence for antiquity—a quality in New York which seems to be honored in the breach rather than the observance. Old Independence Hall is a Fourth-of-July Oration in itself; as is the old bell, with its singularly prophetic inscription.

The Pennsylvania Railroad has made this one of the most delightful routes; and we wish to acknowledge their courtesy in furnishing the cuts which illustrate this article. From Philadelphia the tourist will proceed on his route for Baltimore and Washington.

COLONNADE HOTEL

CHESTNUT AND FIFTEENTH STREETS, PHILADELPHIA.

JOHN CRUMP, Proprietor.   GEO. FREEMAN, Manager.

THE
Congress and Empire Spring Waters
OF SARATOGA

ARE THE BEST OF ALL THE SARATOGA WATERS FOR THE USE OF PERSONS OF CONSTIPATED HABIT.

They act promptly and pleasantly, without producing debility; and their effect is not weakened by continued use, as is the case with ordinary cathartics. At the same time they are not *too* cathartic,—*a fault with some of our more drastic mineral waters*,—but sufficiently so for daily healthful use, and not strong enough to produce reaction.

As an alterative, these waters, by continued use, keep the blood in a very pure and healthful condition, producing a *clear, florid complexion.*

They are especially beneficial in cases of habitual Bilious Headache, Dyspepsia, and Constipation, and are sure preventives of all bilious disorders.

EVERY GENUINE BOTTLE OF CONGRESS WATER HAS A LARGE "C" RAISED ON THE GLASS.

For Sale by Druggists and Hotels throughout the country.
None Genuine Sold on Draught.

At our General Mineral Water Depot in New York all varieties of Natural Waters for sale at proprietors' prices, delivered free in New York, Brooklyn, and Jersey City.

Orders by mail will receive prompt attention. Empties taken back and allowed for at liberal prices. Address,

CONGRESS & EMPIRE SPRING CO.,
Saratoga Springs, N. Y., and
94 Chambers St., New York City.

☞ In connection with a recent Analysis of Congress Water, Prof. C. F. Chandler remarks that "as a *cathartic* water, its almost entire freedom from iron should recommend it above all others."

SARATOGA, LAKE GEORGE, AND PLATTSBURG.

From Albany we take the Rensselaer and Saratoga Railroad (division of the Delaware and Hudson Canal Company) direct to Saratoga, or by way of

TROY, at the head of tide-water, the enterprising city of the Hudson. In fact, it might be considered the *live* town of the river. In the year

TROY HOUSE.
C. H. JONES, Proprietor.

1786, it was called Ferryhook. In 1787, Rensselaerwyck. In the fall of 1787, the settlers began to use the name of Vanderheyden, after the family who owned a great part of the ground where the city now stands. January 9th, 1789, the freeholders of the town met and gave it the name of Troy. As a natural sequence, the adjoining hills took the names of Ida and Olympus.

The best hotel is the "Troy House," corner of First and River Streets, near the steamboat dock, and only a few blocks from the depot.

Free omnibuses to and from the hotel. It is also the most central place in the city, and tourists will always find gentlemanly clerks and kind attention.

Like Troy of old, this city flourishes in an "age of iron." The Bessemer Steel Rail Works, in the southern part of the city, keep up a continual Fourth of July by a display of fireworks that are well worth an evening visit. The manufacture of stoves is also a large part of the business enterprise. We would call attention to the new Empire Heating Range of Swett, Quimby, & Perry, as something new and successful in the way of heating rooms, connected with a fine cooking-range. Troy has also the best reputation for making elegant marbleized mantles. The extensive works of C. W. Billings are situated on the corner of Hutton and North Third Streets; and here we can trace the progress of a slab rough from Hydeville through various manipulations, until it becomes in fact "a thing of beauty." The finest residences in our country are being furnished with mantles of his manufacture. Waters' Paper Boats are also manufactured in Troy. During the last four seasons they have been rowed by the winners of more than a hundred matched races.

The population of Troy is over 50,000, and rapidly growing. The falls of the Poestenkill are in a romantic ravine, within thirty minutes' walk of the Troy House. This stream and the Wynantskill furnish a good water-power. The Union Depot is a fine building; and three railroads centre here—the Hudson River, the Rensselaer and Saratoga, and the Troy and Boston. Taking the

RENSSELAER AND SARATOGA RAILROAD, we cross the Hudson and Green Island, the birthplace of Morrisey, and we believe once used as a camping-ground by General Gates. We pass through the long street of Waterford, and leave Cohoes on our left, a manufacturing town which received its name from the falls of the Mohawk, one of the mouths of which here empties into the Hudson. Its Indian name is said to signify the "Island at the Falls." We pass through Mechanicville, near the historic fields of Stillwater and Bemis Heights; Round Lake Station, with its summer village and camp-meeting privileges, and come to

BALLSTON SPA, twenty-five miles from Troy, a pleasant watering-place, although under the immediate shadow of Saratoga. The best hotel is the "Sans Souci."

We lately came across an article in *Harper's Magazine*, published twenty years ago, which gives a gorgeous description of the youth and beauty that were there assembled; and we were more surprised at the fact that we had a summer hotel that had existed twenty years, than when we met soon after a reference to one of the German Spas in the lines of Spenser's "Faery Queen."

THE BALLSTON ARTESIAN LITHIA SPRING is everywhere noted, and recommended by medical and scientific men as containing the most valuable properties of any spring in our country. The analysis is given in full on another page. It is said that the grandfather of the Hon. Stephen A. Douglas built a log house in Ballston in the year 1792, for the accommodation of invalids.

From Ballston there is a Schenectady Branch Railroad, which materially shortens the distance for those *en route* to Niagara, Sharon, or points west. Seven miles more bring us to

SARATOGA SPRINGS, thirty-two miles from Troy, and one hundred and eighty-two from New York.

SARATOGA SPRINGS.

In our hasty sketch of watering-places and the routes thereto, this great summer resort of our country ought to be printed in large capital letters. The heading deserves a full line of itself, instead of being crowded into a left-hand corner of a page of type—*and it shall have it.* In other words, Saratoga is something more than a *paragraph*, or Barnum would have wheeled it across the continent thirty years ago. Compared with the Springs, other watering-places are mere commas, semi-colons, or, at the most, colons; but this punctuation-point in pleasure-travel is a *full stop.* It is, in fact, a place which every one likes to visit once in a lifetime, and most people once a year.

It pleases a *philosopher* because it is the best place on the continent to study human nature. It pleases the young gentleman and lady of flirting propensities, because they can easily find hearts and heads as soft and responsive as their own. It pleases the managing mother, because she has a field for diplomacy which would puzzle a Richelieu or a Bismarck. It pleases the sporting gentleman, because he has an opportunity of displaying his interest or losing his principal in a fashionable horse-race. It pleases the invalid, for this has been to many a genuine fountain of health. In short, it presents to every condition and character something to be enjoyed; and each class soon attracts its own companions.

PARK OF THE GRAND UNION HOTEL.
BRESLIN, GARDNER, & Co., Proprietors.

Saratoga is like the knight's shield, and can be looked at from either side: one side is the purest gold, and the other tarnished silver. But we will allow each person to do his own moralizing, and proceed with the main object and design of our handbook. The first thing of interest to the stranger is to get located at a hotel. The four finest are

on Broadway, the main street of the village, and we will refer to them in their order, as we approach them from the railroad station.

THE GRAND UNION HOTEL, located on the west side of Broadway, is the largest hotel in Saratoga; and, it is said, larger than any in the world. It not only presents a street frontage of 1364 feet, but also incloses a fine park, a cut of which is here given. The grounds and buildings cover a space seven acres in extent. Its capacious drawing-rooms and dining-halls have been newly adorned and frescoed; and its destiny is secure in the hands of its popular proprietors—Breslin, Gardner, & Co.

CONGRESS HALL.
HATHORN & SOUTHGATE, Proprietors.

CONGRESS HALL is a little to the south, on the opposite side of Broadway, and extends from Spring to Congress Street. It presents a fine architectural front of 416 feet, and its management is complete and satisfactory.

THE GRAND HOTEL, completed in the summer of 1872, is an elegant structure, south of the Grand Union, and on the same side of Broadway. It enjoys the advantage of a fine location, with a piazza frontage of 370 feet, overlooking Congress Spring Park. It is airy and cheerful, and no efforts have been spared to make it one of the finest in this *congerie* of hotels. There are electric bells and clothes-presses in every room, which latter fact will be especially appreciated by the gentler portion of society.

THE GRAND HOTEL.
W. W. LELAND, Proprietor.

THE CLARENDON is situated on a delightful eminence still further to the south; and under its popular and gentlemanly proprietor—Charles

E. Leland, of the "Delavan House," Albany—it has attained the first position in reference to an aristocratic and select class of guests. The celebrated Washington Spring is inclosed in the pleasant grounds connected with the hotel.

STRONG'S REMEDIAL INSTITUTE is the finest health resort in our country, and is not only a Christian home for the sick, but also a grand

DRS. STRONG'S REMEDIAL INSTITUTE.

centre for wealthy, literary, and Christian people. It is the annual summer resort of the Rev. Dr. Cuyler, Robert Carter, and ex-Governor Wells, of Virginia. The most marked features are its homogeneous society, its social life, and its musical entertainments.

The proprietors—Drs. S. S. and S. E. Strong—have become so

CONGRESS SPRING, SARATOGA, IN 1816.

celebrated in their various specialties that leading physicians all over the country recognize the fact that many chronic cases can be treated more effectually in an institution having special appliances than in ordinary practice, and are sending more and more such cases to them for treatment. The senior proprietor has been spending the winter abroad in Paris and in London, giving special attention to the latest researches of the French and English physicians. The house is open all the year, and has no appearance of invalidism.

TEMPLE GROVE SEMINARY (STREET FRONT).

TEMPLE GROVE SEMINARY has a delightful location on what was once called Temple Hill, in the eastern part of the village. The institution is under the efficient management of Charles F. Dowd, A.M., a graduate of Yale College, and well known to the educational world as conducting one of the best Young Ladies' Seminaries in the State. The cuts here given present a fine view of the building. The grounds comprise about one and a half acres, and are covered with a grove of over one hundred native forest trees.

During the winter Saratoga combines all the advantages of a city with the quiet of a country town; for, although the public works and beautiful avenues were constructed mainly for the benefit of summer visitors, they are none the less to the advantage of those who live here in the quiet possession of them from September to June. During the rush of the vacation months, Temple Grove is turned into one of the most delightful summer resorts in Saratoga, and combines the advantages of a commanding position, large and well-shaded grounds, and within five minutes' walk of the Springs. From the Seminary observa-

TEMPLE GROVE SEMINARY (GROVE SIDE).

tory one gets a fine view of the surrounding country for miles in every direction. From the *Saratoga Sun*, edited by our friend Mr. A. S. Pease, we clip the following:—

"Among the institutions of which Saratoga has just reason to be proud is Temple Grove Seminary. Under the excellent and skillful management of Professor Dowd, this Seminary has attained not only a State but a National eminence. Among the pupils are young ladies from all points of the United States, and the reputation of the Seminary is steadily increasing. The scholarship of the graduates of Temple Grove has for several years been of marked excellence. No department of mental or general culture seems to be neglected, but everything that contributes to a perfect education is carefully regarded by the Principal, and inwrought, as it were, into the character of the pupil. Not only is Professor Dowd to be congratulated on his notable success, but Saratoga Springs possesses no institution of which she ought to feel more proud or prize more highly than Temple Grove Seminary."

The most prominent Springs in and about Saratoga, and those best known for the excellence of their mineral properties, are the Congress, the Empire, the High Rock, the Star, the Excelsior, and the Geyser.

CONGRESS SPRING was discovered in 1792, by a party of gentlemen who were engaged in hunting in the vicinity. One of these gentlemen was an ex-member of Congress, from Exeter, New Hampshire, and the name of Congress was complimentarily bestowed. Since then, its name has become familiar in every civilized country. The old picture of the Spring, as it appeared in 1816, presents a great contrast to the present pavilion and surroundings of Congress Park. It has a decided advantage in being handy to the various hotels; but we would cite the following incident as a gentle caution to rashness and new arrivals. It was attributed to John G. Saxe, in the summer of 1872. A lady returning from the Spring one morning, met the poet and said, with great gusto, "Good morning, Mr. Saxe; I have just drank six glasses of Congress Water."— His response was at once kind and expressive: "Don't let me detain you, madam."

THE EMPIRE SPRING is situated near the base of a high limestone bluff, about three-fourths of a mile from the Congress Spring. It was called, for a long time, the New Congress, as its general qualities closely resemble the Congress; but it has lately attracted the attention of medical men, as it possesses valuable properties which are adapted to the successful treatment of lung complaints.

THE HIGH ROCK is the only spring in Saratoga which seemed independent of tubing and masonry, and ages ago built a curb for itself. It

CONGRESS SPRING AND PARK, AND COLUMBIAN SPRING, 1873.

was the first discovered, and was a deer resort long before Saratoga was made happy by a hotel. The first white man on record who tasted these waters was Sir William Johnston, in the year 1767. Our cut furnishes a good aboriginal idea of Saratoga and its great healing rock in the wilderness. The mound is about three or four feet high, and is certainly a great curiosity. The geologist and the chemist finds here a subject for reflection and analysis, and it carries them far back into a

SARATOGA HIGH ROCK, 1767.

pre-historic past. It is, indeed, a venerable mound; but the water still bubbles up as brightly as when the bursting of its gas-cells broke only on the stillness of the wildwood. One thing is certain—there is more poetry in High Rock than any other fountain in the country. It has been known for centuries as the "great medicine spring;" and many of those who to-day gather under its pleasant pavilion, give it the preference over later rivals.

GEYSER SPRING, SARATOGA.

The Saratoga Star Spring has the finest bottling-house in Saratoga, and is located between the High Rock and the Empire. It has been known for nearly a century, and is one of the most popular to-day throughout New England. This company was among the first to inaugurate the system of sending the water in kegs and barrels, supplying families and druggists at one-fourth the cost. The present superintendent—Melvin Wright (like the ancestors of *Thursty McQuill*)—had the honor of being born in one of the pleasantest villages in Vermont, and is therefore a representative, in more senses than one, of "the Star that never sets."

The Excelsior Spring has a charming location, about a mile east of the village, and has a romantic walk the entire distance, leading through forest trees. It is, in fact, the finest stroll in Saratoga for lovers of Nature and lovers generally. The Spring has been a great success in the hands of its enterprising proprietors, A. R. Lawrence & Co. The large and commodious bottling-house is located in the centre of Excelsior Park—that portion of Saratoga known for many years as the "Valley of the Ten Springs." The Excelsior Lake, a beautiful sheet of water, with sloping banks adorned by lofty trees, also adds its charms to the place. The more elevated portions of Excelsior Park have been divided into large and small villa plots, many of which command fine views of the mountains in Vermont and the Lake George Hills; and we believe that the attention of the public has only to be called to the lots now offered for sale in Excelsior Park to make this beautiful spot soon vie with the environs of New York in its villa homes and tasteful cottages.

The Geyser Spring—Vail, Batcheller & Adams, proprietors—is located on the Ballston Road, one and a half miles south of the principal hotels, and is one of the great curiosities of this mineral valley. It was discovered in February, 1870, and developed by experimental drilling in the solid rock. The vein was struck by the drill in the bird's-eye limestone, one hundred and forty feet beneath the surface rock, and the water immediately commenced spouting at the surface, being forced up by the pressure of its own carbonic acid gas, spouting through an inch nozzle to the height of thirty feet. The grounds about the Geyser

VIEW OF EXCELSIOR SPRING, AND A PORTION OF EXCELSIOR PARK.

Spring are very picturesque and beautiful. On the Geyser premises is a handsome lake, covering about sixty acres, and over one mile in length; also a handsome waterfall of twenty-two feet, with ravines, terraces, shady and cool retreats to welcome the visitor.

There is a line of stages which run every half hour between the principal hotels and the Spring, for the accommodation of visitors. The fact that this Spring is located 140 feet beneath a solid rock renders it free from all impurities of surface waters, which accounts for its uniform taste and clearness.

POINTS OF INTEREST.—Saratoga has many places of interest in its immediate vicinity. Saratoga Lake, with its "legend;" and "Moon's House;" "Chapman Hill," with its charming view; Wagman's Hill, about three miles beyond; Haggerty Hill, six miles north of the village; and Lake Lovely, on the boulevard to Saratoga Lake. For further particulars we refer the tourist to the neat handbook of "Saratoga, and How to See It," published by Mr. R. F. Dearborn, and sold at all the news-stands and Springs in the village.

ADIRONDACK COMPANY'S RAILROAD.—This route to the Adirondacks and Lake George is one of the most popular excursions to be taken from Saratoga. The traveler by this route passes through the romantic and picturesque valley of the Upper Hudson—through King's, South Corinth, Jessup's Landing to Hadley, the railroad station for Luzerne, a charming village at the junction of the Hudson and the Sacandaga. "Rockwell's Hotel" is known to all the sojourners and guests of Saratoga as the place to secure a game dinner, a dish of trout, and a "taste" of the wilderness.

Pursuing the railroad, we pass through Stony Creek to Thurman, thirty-six miles from Saratoga Springs, at the junction of the Schroon River and the Hudson, and the station for parties *en route* for Lake George or Warrensburgh. Stages connect for these points on the arrival of the train. This stage route to Lake George is over a fine plank-road, and the same in distance as the route from Glen's Falls. The next stations above Thurman are the Glen, forty-four miles; and Riverside, fifty miles from Saratoga. At Riverside persons leave the cars for Chester, Pottersville, Schroon Lake, Johnsburg, and other points north. Schroon Lake, with its popular hotel, the "Leland House," is only ten miles from the station. North Creek is fifty-seven miles from Saratoga. This railroad opens up a country rich in mineral resources, and attractive in romantic and picturesque scenery.

RENSSELAER AND SARATOGA RAILROAD, CONTINUED.— Pursuing our northern route from Saratoga, we pass through Gansevoort and Moreau to Fort Edward; and the branch railroad brings us to

THE ROCKWELL HOUSE, GLEN'S FALLS, N. Y.

GLEN'S FALLS, the flourishing and enterprising town of northern New York. The streets are finely laid out, and well shaded. The soldier's monument and new Music Hall testify to the taste, intelligence, and public spirit of the place.

The Rockwell House, just completed, a cut of which is here given, is quite as complete in all its appointments as any hotel in the State. The rooms are all spacious and airy, and an atmosphere of home and comfort pervades the entire establishment. The gentlemanly proprietors, the Rockwell Brothers, are well known among tourists and travelers. Educated in this "art of arts" by one who has made our own *Luzerne*, at the meeting of the Sacandaga and the Hudson, quite as well known and reverently regarded as the classic Luzerne of Switzerland. Conveyances can be had at all times to Lake George, and stages leave morning and evening. Persons arriving on the evening train thus have a good night's rest, and a pleasant morning ride to the Lake. Glen's Falls is surrounded by so much of historic interest and beautiful scenery that it demands even from the hurried traveler more than a passing glance. This is the central point, as it were, about which our great novelist grouped the scenes of "The Last of the Mohicans." A short distance from the village the Hudson River makes a descent of 72 feet in a succession of leaps over rugged rocks; and here is the famous cave so graphically described by Cooper. The width of the river at this point is about 900 feet.

To LAKE GEORGE. From Glens Falls a fine plank road passes through a beautiful country. It is well built and always smooth, and seems like a highway to some city rather than an excursion route for summer travel. On the way we pass Bloody Pond, on the right, and a monument to Col. Williams, on the left. Lake George is a place where one goes with the idea of staying two or three days, and then— stays two or three weeks. The charming scenery and cheerful Hotel (the Fort William Henry) present perhaps the strongest combination to be found in our country of immediate beauty and comfort. Near the Hotel are the ruins of old Fort William Henry, telling a sad history of the past. About a mile to the south-east are the ruins of Fort George. It has been christened about as many times as the Hudson, and like the Hudson has retained its prosiest name. The Iroquois called it Andiata-rocte (the lake that shuts itself in); by other tribes Canidere-oit (the tail of the Lake, as a part of Lake Champlain). Father Jaques, traversing it in 1646, during the festival of Corpus

FORT WILLIAM HENRY HOTEL, LAKE GEORGE.

T. ROESSLE & SON, PROPRIETORS.

ALSO OF THE

Arlington House, Washington, D. C.

Christi, called it Lac Sacrament. Sir William Johnson, serving his king with greater zeal than his country, styled it Lake George. Its most poetical name was Horicon—of uncertain origin, said to signify silvery water. Lake George combines various attractions. It has something of interest for every one—the lover of history, of romance, of beauty, and lovers generally (as a friend remarks, not confined to inanimate objects). But we believe the greatest attraction is in the unwritten poetry which lives among these scattered islands. A graceful little steamboat makes a daily trip to and from Ticonderoga. The islands are said to be the same in number as the days of the year, and we think one might find a small rock extra for leap year.

PRINCIPAL ISLANDS.

Two miles down the Lake Tea Island, next Diamond; Long Island, 12 miles from Caldwell; Dome Island, Recluse Island. After Bolton Landing we come to "14-mile Island;" Shelving Rock on the east, and Tongue Mountain opposite. (These form the entrance to the Narrows.) This is the most picturesque portion of the Lake; it is at this place 400 feet deep. Sabbath Day Point, (where Gen. Abercrombie landed, on his way to attack the French one Sabbath morning), Bluff Point, Odell Island, Scotch Bonnet, Anthony's Nose, on the east; and Rogers' Slide on the west.

Persons en route for Plattsburgh, Rouse's Point, Montreal, or the North Woods, may make the detour from the main route to Glen's Falls and Caldwell Landing, and down the lake to Ticonderoga, and connect with steamer on Lake Champlain. Unless time is a great consideration, the "Rockwell House," "Fort William Henry," and "Lake George" ought not to be left out of a summer excursion. The steamers on the lake are fitted and furnished in every particular to the wants of the pleasure-seeker; and, in addition to regular daily trips, are subject to charter by pleasure parties for excursions among the bays and islands for which Lake George is so justly famous.

Returning now to the main line, which we left at Fort Edward, we pass north through **Dunham's Basin, Smith's Basin, Fort Ann, and Comstock's Landing,** to

WHITEHALL, at the head of Lake Champlain. The romantic surroundings of the village, and the cottage houses almost hanging on the hillside, give it decidedly the appearance of a foreign town. It has a location quite like an infant Chicago, and is the head centre of the lumber trade on Lake Champlain.

"Hall's Hotel" is located in the central and business part of the village,—a convenient house for persons traveling either on business or pleasure. A cut of it is here given.

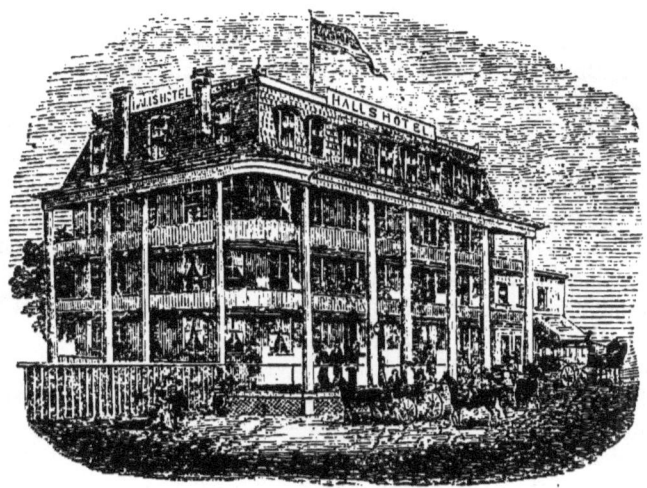

HALL'S HOTEL, WHITEHALL, N. Y.

From Whitehall two routes now open to the north, *via* the Lake Champlain steamers and *via* cars to Rutland; and we will refer to them both in brief.

LAKE CHAMPLAIN ROUTE.—This beautiful lake is 120 miles in length, almost due north and south, and is the natural continuation of the Hudson River Valley. New England was, in fact, for some years considered an island; and indeed it is only three or four miles between some of the tributaries of the Hudson and Lake Champlain. The lake lies between the Adirondacks and the Green Mountains, and presents some of the finest views, and has special interest to the student of history. Soon after leaving the narrow and devious channel, the tourist will notice South Bay on the left, memorable for the route of the ill-fated Baron Diesquieu, in 1755. A run of twenty miles brings us to the remarkable ruins of Ticonderoga, on a high rocky cliff at the confluence of the outlet of Lake George with the waters of Champlain. Passing the ruins of the fortress of Crown Point, now in the last stages of decay, the lake begins to expand, and nine miles bring us to Westport. Three miles onward we pass the beautiful village of Essex and the Four Brother islands, where Arnold fought his last battle with Carleton. We pass Shelburne Bay on the right, and almost in the track of the steamer rises a high conical rock,—the "Great Rock Reggio," celebrated in colonial annals, and believed to have been—long before the days of Champlain—established by treaty as the boundary between the Mohawks and their hereditary enemies the Algonquins.

Burlington is a beautiful city, having a fine location, and one of the most popular hotels in Vermont—the "Van Ness House." We refer to Burlington again in our article on Montreal and the Thousand Islands. After touching at Port Kent, we run three miles, and find ourselves abreast of the delta of Ausable River, a singularly beautiful and romantic stream. Passing Valcour Straits and Garden Island, we come to

PLATTSBURGH, pleasantly situated on both banks of the Saranac River, at the foot of Cumberland Bay. This is the great starting-point for the Adirondacks and the North Woods. The "Fouquet House" makes it a delightful threshold *en route* for the wilderness. The ornamental grounds of the hotel show the taste of the gentlemanly proprietor, Louis Fouquet. The new building, a cut of which is here given, is an elegant and spacious structure, not less imposing by its dimensions and position than attractive by the novelty and beauty of its architecture. It is capable of accommodating one hundred and fifty guests, and the rooms are large and supplied with every requisite of comfort and enjoyment.

FOUQUET'S HOTEL, PLATTSBURG, N. Y.

Plattsburgh was rendered memorable during the war of 1812, by brilliant naval and military victories, of which it was the theatre. The Ausable Chasm, a view of which is here given, may be visited from Plattsburgh by a drive of about twelve miles over a road which for several miles runs directly on the margin of the lake. There is also a fine trip by steamer to be taken to St. Albans, with its magnificent hotel — the "Welden House." In short, a week can be agreeably spent in the vicinity of Plattsburgh.

The Champlain by daylight is a pleasant excursion. It connects at Ticonderoga for Lake George, each way; at Whitehall with Rensselaer and Saratoga Railroad; at Burlington with Vermont Central for Mount Mansfield and White Mountains; at Port Kent for Keeseville; at Plattsburgh for the Adirondack Sporting Region; at Rouse's Point for Alburgh Springs, Montreal, Quebec, and Ogdensburgh.

THE ADIRONDACKS.—This great northern wilderness is nearly a hundred miles in diameter, and the whole region is intersected and diversified by a network of lakes and streams. These systems of water communication afford very convenient means of transit for hunters and pleasure-seekers. The majority of tourists start directly for Lower Saranac Lake or St. Regis, and thence make various trips to the lakes and mountains. The most picturesque route probably is *via* Whiteface Mountain, up the west branch of the Ausable River from Point of Rocks. Splendid views are obtained from the summit of Whiteface Mountain, including fine views of Mount Marcy, Mount Seward, Nipple Top, and the whole range of the Adirondacks; and, in the other direction, the glimmering thread of the St. Lawrence is traced along the horizon, and to the north the spires of Montreal may be discerned. Sixty-four different bodies of water — lakes, ponds, and rivers — are visible by the naked eye from this mountain; and, with a glass, quite a good many more. In fact, the number might be materially increased by the number of glasses. But we will leave the tourist in the hands of guides more competent than any written description, and allow him to pursue his way unmolested for **Montreal, the White Mountains, or Niagara.**

THE AUSABLE CHASM.

LAKE CHAMPLAIN STEAMERS.

The Fashionable Thoroughfare and Pleasure Route between New York and Montreal.

VERMONT, ... Capt. *Wm. H. Flagg.*
ADIRONDACK, ... " *Wm. Anderson.*
UNITED STATES, ... " *Geo. Rushlow.*
OAKES AMES, ... " *B. J Holt.*

☞ Forming two lines daily (Sundays excepted) between

WHITEHALL AND ROUSES POINT.

CONNECTIONS:

At Whitehall, with trains of Rensselaer and Saratoga R. R., for Saratoga, Troy, Albany, New York, and all Southern and Western points.

At Ticonderoga, with steamer Minnehaha, through Lake George.

At Burlington, with trains of Vermont Central Railroad, for all Eastern points, and the Mountains of Vermont and New Hampshire.

At Port Kent, with stages for Keeseville.

At Plattsburgh, with trains of New York and Canada Railroad, for the Hunting and Fishing localities of the Saranac Lakes and the Adirondack Wilderness.

At Rouses Point, with trains of O. & L. C. and Grand Trunk Railways for Ogdensburg, Montreal, Quebec, and all points in Northern New York and Canada.

☞ Tickets and information furnished at the principal agencies of the Erie, New York Central, Hudson River, and Grand Trunk Railroads, in New York, Philadelphia, Baltimore, St. Louis, Chicago, Niagara Falls, Montreal; also at the Home Office of the Hudson River Day Line, and on board the Hudson River steamers, and at all the principal stations of all connecting lines.

The Steamers composing the Line are, as they always have been, models of excellence, neatness and comfort, combining all modern improvements, and every attention is paid by their officers to the patrons of the route.

A. L. INMAN, General Sup't.

MONTREAL AND THE THOUSAND ISLANDS.

From Whitehall, as we before stated, there are two routes to the north, one of which we have just sketched; the other now awaits our consideration.

The "Rensselaer and Saratoga Railroad," after leaving Whitehall, bends to the east, and passes through the villages of Fairhaven and Hydeville, with their well-known slate quarries. The one near the depot at Fairhaven, is conducted by Mr. R. C. Colburn; and the one at Hydeville, by the Forest Mining Company. Hydeville is pleasantly situated. Lake Bomoseen affords good fishing, and is only a mile from the village. Passing through Castleton and West Rutland, we come to

RUTLAND, 244 miles from New York. This is the centre of the great marble-trade, and the railroad centre of Vermont. The pleasant and popular hotel, the "Bardwell House," is handy to the station, and is well known throughout New York and New England for its generous and hospitable management. There are pleasant drives in every direction, especially the route to the *Clarendon* and the *Middletown Healing Springs*. Taking the

RUTLAND DIVISION OF THE VERMONT CENTRAL RAILROAD, we pass north through Sutherland Falls, Pittsford, Brandon, Leicester Junction, and Salisbury, to

MIDDLEBURY, with its pleasant hotel, the "Addison House." From this point there is a fine drive to Lake Dunmore. The next stations to the north are Brooksville, New Haven, and Vergennes—the oldest city in Vermont. We now pass Ferrisburgh, North Ferrisburgh, Charlotte, and Shelburne, to

BURLINGTON, which we saw in our last article, with its pleasant location on the lake. It rises in natural terraces, something like Newburgh, on the Hudson. From the college tower, or dome, a wide extended view is obtained of the city and lake, and the distant Adirondacks; to the north the meadow lands of the winding Winooski; to the east the Nose and Chin of Mount Mansfield. The summer visitor at Burlington will find himself within easy distance of a number of delightful resorts.

The "Van Ness House" is a fine hotel, central in location, with a nice outlook upon lake and mountain. It is the largest in Burlington, and will rank as one of the most convenient and thoroughly appointed

VAN NESS HOUSE.
D. C. BARDEN & Co., Proprietors.

houses in New England. Resuming our railway journey for the north, we pass through Essex, Milton, Georgia, and minor stations, to

ST. ALBANS.—This village is situated about two miles from, and overlooks Lake Champlain. It is a town of about 7,000 inhabitants, and was made famous during the rebellion by a Canadian raid. It is a central point for persons *en route* for Alburgh and Shelden Springs, and has a large and magnificent hotel—the "Welden House,"—a cut of which is given on opposite page.

Its reputation as a pleasant and attractive place of summer resort, as well as an agreeable and comfortable house at all times for travelers, is not surpassed in New England. It contains over two hundred rooms, and is admirably arranged for private families.

"The panoramic views from St. Albans are among the finest in th world. Aldis Hill, spoken of in 'Norwood,' is within one-half mile of

THOMAS LAVENDER, PROPRIETOR.

the Welden House, and the summit of Bellevue, accessible by an easy carriage road, is within two miles, commanding on the east a view of Mansfield and Jay, besides a wide reach of mountain, valley, hill, and plain, adorned with lovely farms and villages; on the west a magnificent view of the Adirondacks, besides a hundred miles of Lake Champlain, dotted with sails, broken with islands, and bounded by a wide stretch of as lovely a country as the eye ever beheld; while on the north the vision rests on Canada, the Richelieu and St. Lawrence Rivers.

ALBURGH SPRINGS are situated on the railroad to Rouse's Point, seventeen miles from St. Albans. The pleasant hotel—the "Alburgh Springs House,"—on the banks of the beautiful Missisquoi Bay, is a fine centre for enjoying lake, highland, or quiet village life, with facilities for boating, shooting, and fishing. Persons *en route* for Montreal may now pursue their journey *via* Rouse's Point, or return and go *via* St. Albans. Three hours' run from St. Albans bring us to

MONTREAL, 420 miles from New York. It is situated on the south side of an island, thirty miles in length and ten miles in greatest breadth. The tourist will first locate himself at the "St. Lawrence

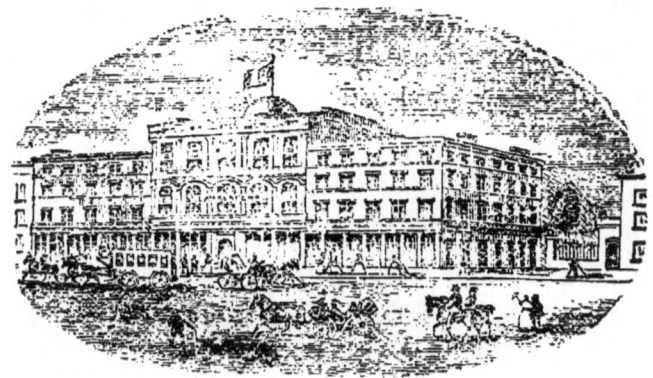

ST. LAWRENCE HALL.
F. GERIKEN, Proprietor.

Hall," and put himself in substantial preparation for seeing one of the finest cities of the new world. This hotel is the largest and most central in the city, being capable of accommodating five hundred guests. During the past winter it has been entirely refurnished, and several improvements made. Old guests will still recognize the pleasant countenances and superior management of Mr. C. R. Chadwick, formerly with Mr. Hogan; and Mr. J. T. Burkholder, formerly of the "Rossin House," Toronto.

Montreal has a pleasing appearance, and seems to be a happy city.

It makes a pleasant northern terminus to our route, and has many places of interest to be visited; Notre Dame Cathedral, the Church of the Jesuits, St. Patrick's, the Victoria Bridge, and fine drives about Mount Royal. This mountain is one thousand feet in height, and gives its name to the island city. Among the different mercantile establishments, we mention Savage, Lyman & Co., jewellers, house established in 1818; and the famous Recollet House, Brown & Claggett, proprietors. There is a marked civility of Montreal citizens toward strangers, and every one carries away with them *something which is not dutiable*, viz., the pleasantest of recollections.

NOBBY ISLAND.

THE THOUSAND ISLANDS.—The shortest route to the Thousand Islands is *via* Albany and Watertown; but we consider the route *via* Montreal the pleasantest, and therefore speak of them in this connection. The Thousand Islands—eighteen hundred in reality—extend about forty miles, and vary in size from a few feet in diameter to three hundred acres. The general average, we should say, would be about three or four acres, and all are beautifully shaded and wooded. The idea of building on these islands was first conceived by Mr. George Pullman, of palace-car fame, who, some ten years ago, purchased one of these islands, and erected thereon a temporary cottage. In the summer of 1870, Mr. Henry R. Heath, of New York City, and Mr. Charles S. Goodwin, of Oneida, New York, purchased the first island situated below Pullman Island, and known as Nobby Island, from a large rock near the water's edge resembling the knob of a door. In the summer of 1871 they erected a modern Gothic cottage, with docks, flag-staff, &c., a cut of which is here given. Now the islands, on every side, are being improved and built upon.

There is probably no river or lake in the world more romantic and delightful than this section of the St. Lawrence; and we imagine these islands furnish a good foundation for a *rural Venice*. During the summer of 1872, President Grant and family, General Phil. Sheridan, &c., were domiciled nearest neighbors to Nobby Island.

The "Thousand Island House," Alexandria Bay, N. Y., is a fine hotel, and will accommodate six hundred guests. This bay is thirty miles from Cape Vincent, and thirty-six from Ogdensburgh. Persons making the round trip, *via* Niagara Falls, always make a point to take in the Thousand Islands and the Rapids of the St. Lawrence.

THE RAPIDS.—The first rapid below Ogdensburgh is near Chimney Island; the next, the rapids of the Long Sault, nine miles in length. Here the river runs twenty miles an hour. Then the Coteau Rapids, below Grand Island; then the Lachine Rapids, below the town of Lachine, only nine miles from Montreal.

Our routes have now carried us through a good part of the Empire State, and as we turn aside for a moment to New England and its representative mountains, we think we are justified in saying that no State in the Union presents so fine a landscape and such a framework of beauty as New York. We will call the *picture* a bird's-eye view of Lake George, the Adirondacks, Otsego Lake, Lake Seneca, and Watkins Glen. We will call the *framework* the Hudson River, Lake Champlain, the River St. Lawrence, Lake Ontario, and Niagara Falls.

THE WHITE AND GREEN MOUNTAINS.

No Tourist Guide of the Hudson would be complete without giving the route to the Green Hills of Vermont and the White Hills of New Hampshire, for a large part of the travel to these mountains generally goes one way, *via* the Hudson River and Saratoga.

MANCHESTER is one of the finest villages in Vermont, at the foot of Mount Equinox, in the very heart of the Green Mountains. The

EQUINOX HOUSE.
F. H. Orvis, Proprietor.

"Equinox House" has a wide reputation, and is one of the most successful in our country. During the last winter F. H. Orvis, its popular proprietor, conducted with marked success the "St. James Hotel," of Jacksonville, Florida. He is once more on his native heath, prepared to make Manchester, for the season of 1873, one of the finest resorts in the United States.

The "Vanderlip House" is also in the central part of this pleasant village, and has enjoyed for more than a quarter of a century the reputation of a first-class and home-like hotel. The rooms are high and airy, dining-rooms large and pleasant, and the parlor some sixty feet by forty. The grounds are nicely shaded, and from the windows there is a fine view of the mountains. This hotel is kept open also during

VANDERLIP HOUSE.
E. M. Vanderlip, Proprietor.

the winter. The "Elm House" has a pleasant location, and has recently undergone thorough and extensive repairs. The Burr & Burton Seminary is a very successful institution, and has a fine outlook upon village, valley, and mountain.

Persons en route for Manchester may go via day-line to Hudson; thence by cars, and arrive the same evening; or via Albany and Troy, taking Troy and Boston Railroad to Bennington, and Harlem Extension to Manchester; also, via Saratoga and Rutland, and down the Harlem Extension about thirty miles. A direct route is also furnished from New York via Harlem and Harlem Extension Railroad.

Middletown Springs are situated on the Poultney River, a small

MONTVERT HOTEL, Middletown Springs, Vt.

tributary stream to Lake Champlain. The village lies nestled among the green hills of Vermont, and is famous as a quiet and healthful summer resort. It has a magnificent and commodious hotel—the "Montvert,"—a cut of which is here given: Mr. Dwight Doolittle, proprietor. Persons *en route* for Middletown may go *via* Rutland, or *via* Troy and Troy and Boston Railroad to Poultney, on the Rutland and Washington Division. Either way admits of a fine carriage drive.

MOUNT MANSFIELD is the most prominent elevation of the Green Mountain range, and can easily be reached *via* Burlington and Water-

MOUNT MANSFIELD HOTEL, STOWE, VT.

bury, on the Vermont Central Railroad. Stowe, at the foot of the mountains, is a pleasant place of summer resort.

Brattleboro, with its new hotel—the "Brooks House,"—and Bellows Falls, with its "Island House," are on the eastern side of the Green Mountain range, and are pleasant resting-places, in the Connecticut River Valley.

THE WHITE MOUNTAINS.—Persons *en route* for the White Mountains take the cars or boat *via* Rutland and Burlington, and proceed *via*

Vermont Central to White River Junction. Stop over, if weary, at the "Junction House;" and resume the route *via* Wells River, Littleton, and Bethlehem, to the "Twin Mountain House," a cut of which is here given. We hope, however, to have a better representation of this pleasant hotel for our next edition, as it is in reality one of the finest in New Hampshire. For two seasons it has been the resort of the Rev. Henry Ward Beecher. From this point parties can diverge to all points about the Mountains. The "Crawford House" is only nine

A. T. & O. F. BARRON, PROPRIETORS.

miles distant; the "Profile," sixteen; the "Waumbeck," eleven; the "Glen House," thirty.

The route to the "Summit" is now made easy by the Mount Washington Railway. The Boston, Concord, Montreal, and White Mountain Railroad Company have pushed their line into the very heart of the White Mountains, and the route can now be made in half the time, compared with the long stage-lines of ten or twelve years ago. The summit of Mount Washington is 6,285 feet above the level of the sea; and we will leave you there, safe and secure, beyond even the reach of a rhetorical sentence.

ALBURGH SPRINGS HOUSE,

AT ALBURGH SPRINGS, GRAND ISLE CO., VERMONT,

Sixteen miles North of St. Albans, on the line of the Vermont Central Railroad.

H. H. HOWE, Proprietor.   (Late of the American Hotel, Burlington, Vt.)

D. S. CUTTING, Clerk.

Post-office Address, Alburgh Springs, Vermont.

This house, on the banks of the beautiful MISSISQUOI BAY, at the northern extremity of Lake Champlain, is one mile from the Railroad. Those who are seeking health and a quiet resort for the summer, will find here combined attractions, at once varied and unique. Mountain air, fine views of lake and highlands, and quiet village life, scenery both picturesque and grand, with facilities for **Boating, Shooting,** and **Fishing,** all add their healthful influences to recuperate the weary dweller and worker in the city; while the famous Alburgh Spring—itself a fountain of health and strength—is inclosed in the grounds of the hotel. For nearly a century this Spring has been the resort of invalids, and some of those healed by it forty years ago, regularly visit it every year. For all diseases of the skin or internal organs, arising from impurity of blood, or deficient nervous power, the water has proved a reliable remedy.

Internal Tumors, Calculi, etc.; hopeless cases of Humors, Chronic Rheumatism, Liver and Kidney Complaints, Scrofula, Dyspepsia, Catarrh, etc., etc.,

have yielded to it; and many persons, given over by skillful physicians, have here found, in NATURE'S OWN REMEDY, relief from suffering, and restoration to strength.

To these great natural advantages, the **Alburgh Springs House** adds the comforts of a good Hotel, elegantly furnished, and the quiet of a country home. Guests will be received after May 1st.

EASTMAN BUSINESS UNIVERSITY.
President's Office and Practical Departments,
Corner Washington and Mill Streets, Poughkeepsie, N. Y.

[OVER.]

Eastman Business University.

POUGHKEEPSIE, N. Y., ON-THE-HUDSON.

A Practical School for the Times!

Training Young Men and Boys for a Successful Start in Life—Teaching them How to Make a Living and for Becoming Active Business Men.

Sixteen years ago Mr. Eastman established the first **Business College** in America, introducing a system of **Practical Training** that has since educated more than **Eighteen Thousand** of the present **prosperous business men** of the country. It is beginning to be understood that a man to succeed, become **eminent**, or a **leader in his business** or **profession** must be **practically educated.**— The good sense that is now pervading the minds of the American people on this subject is evinced by the large patronage this Institution is enjoying from every section of the country.

It is not simply a school for the merchant, but the course of study is so arranged as to be of incalculable advantage to all classes of the community, the **Farmer** as well as the **Merchant**, the **Lawyer** as well as the **Banker.** Its specialty is to prepare **Boys, Young and Middle-aged Men** in the shortest time and at the least expense for the active duties of life, **teach them how to get a living, make money, and become enterprising useful citizens.** It does nothing more and nothing less. How well it has succeeded is best known to its thousands of graduates and patrons, to be found in every town in the land.

There are in this country to-day thousands of parents whose greatest concern is the **prosperity of their sons** that are just starting in active life, and to them especially, is presented the claims of this Institu-

A FEW FACTS

IN REGARD TO

Eastman College.

1st, Its Character. It is a *live, practical, common sense school*—conducted by *able, skillful teachers* and is endorsed by the *most prominent Educators and Business men of the country.*

2d, Its Location. It is located in the *famous city of Schools and Churches*—the most populous, beautiful and healthful city on the Hudson between New York and Albany.

3d, Its Standing. It is the *oldest, largest patronized and only practical* business training school in the country, and stands to day the *acknowledged head for imparting a thorough commercial education.*

4th, Course of Study. The course of study is *short, practical, useful and reasonable.* It is *just* what every man *needs and will use,* no matter what his *calling or profession is to be.*

5th, Assisting Graduates. It is the only institution that assists its graduates to situations on completing the course. A large business acquaintance, which extends to almost every village and city in the United States, together with the reputation the College enjoys, enables us to provide situations for all who merit and desire them.

6th, Time of Entering. Applicants are admitted any week day in the year. There is no class system, each student receiving individual instruction. There are no examinations at commencement Boys past the age of 14 years, young men and men of all ages are admitted.

7th, Terms. Tuition for the *Business Course, time unlimited* $45 00, with a matriculation fee of $5 00. Board in best private families from $4.00 to $5.00 per week. *The total expense of Tuition, Board and Stationery* for the prescribed course of three months is from $110 to $125. Students selecting cheaper boarding places can complete the course at much less expense. *A deduction from the above is made* when two or more enter from the same place at the same time. (See Catalogue.)

NOTE.—We invite *business men, parents and young men* to make a personal examination of the Institution, its original and pre eminent course of study and plan of operation, confident that it will meet their fullest expectations.

The Illustrated College Journal giving a history of the Institution, practical course of study, and plan of operation, and the College Directory, giving the names, addresses and business of over 3,000 graduates who owe their present success to the Institution, may be had by addressing the President, H. G. EASTMAN, LL.D., Poughkeepsie, N. Y.

[OVER.]

OPINIONS FROM EMINENT SOURCES.

Rev. S. D. Burchard, D.D., *Pastor 13th Street Presbyterian Church, New York, says:*

"Dr. H. G. EASTMAN:

"DEAR SIR: Having just returned from a visit to your practical College, where I was made familiar with its workings, I take pleasure in expressing my convictions of its character and usefulness. In the first place, the conception of such an Institution including the THEORY and PRACTICE of Business, qualifying young men in the shortest possible time for business in all its scopes and details, is honor enough for any one man, and worthy the age in which we live. Your plan of instruction, so unique and comprehensive, so facile and free from the toil and drudgery of ordinary schools; and then your genius, inspiring all and presiding over all, have contributed to make your Institution what it is, the most successful of modern improvements, a monument of your talent, and a blessing to the land. I know of no institution, either in the old or new world, that receives or is worthy of a patronage so extended as this. Very respectfully yours,

"S. D. BURCHARD."

From **D. T. Moore,** *of "Moore's Rural New Yorker," of New York City:*

"H. G. Eastman, L.L.D., President of Eastman College, has been elected Mayor of the City of Poughkeepsie by an overwhelming majority. He is a man *who has achieved success by industry and goaheadativeness in building up a great, successful, and useful institution on the Hudson.* We are glad to chronicle the fact that such a man is honored by his fellow citizens."

Mr. Montfort, *of the Cincinnati Presbytery, July 6th,* 1871, *says:*

"Our children are stuffed with too much Latin and Classical Literature for the great practicabilities of active, busy life. You (Mayor Eastman) have hit the nail on the centre, and your Institution cannot be too extensively known."

From **Henry Ward Beecher's** *Paper, the Christian Union:*

"We know of this Institution (Eastman College) and *its admirable results within the circle of our personal acquaintance* and we cordially recommend any one who wants what it offers, to go there for it, confident that it will be the best of the kind."

☞ See Catalogue for many hundred similar ones. Sent free to any address.

NECTAR SYRUP,

or,

A SODA-FOUNTAIN AT HOME.

CREAM-NECTAR.—By this name is known one of the most delicious and invigorating beverages, in which carbonic acid gas enters as one of the chief elements. It is this gas which produces the sparkle and brisk fermentation of Champagne and the Mineral Waters. In the Nectar it is so retained that *none escapes* during effervescence.

During warm weather it is the best cooling beverage that can be used, and hence every family should keep it on hand.

The best cooling and invigorating drinks, for the warm weather, are made from NECTAR SYRUP. A goblet, a little syrup, a teaspoonful or two of sugar, and some cool water, are all that is necessary to produce an excellent beverage—like lemonade—restoring the exhausted or debilitated energies of the system at once, without the trouble of making from the fruit. Try it.

THE SYRUP OF CREAM-NECTAR is prepared and put up in convenient packages, so that every family can keep on hand a supply for immediate use—one bottle costing only fifty cents—makes from ten to twelve glasses of *Cream-Nectar*, or about fifty glasses of superior lemonade. Hence it is the most economical as well as the most pleasant and healthy beverage in the market. It can be used for all the purposes of Lemon Syrup.

TRAVELERS! take with you a small bottle of NECTAR SYRUP. It can be easily put in your satchel; and, when warm, tired, and thirsty, put a couple of teaspoonfuls of the Syrup and about as much sugar in the glass of water you are about to drink; it will add very much to your comfort.

For sale by all grocers. Orders addressed to

WELSH & REYNOLDS,

P. O. Box 79.   JERSEY CITY, N. J.

NARRAGANSETT STEAMSHIP CO.

AND OLD COLONY R. R.
"FALL RIVER LINE"
BETWEEN
NEW YORK and BOSTON, via NEWPORT and FALL RIVER.

STEAMERS LEAVE NEW YORK AT

5 P. M. DAILY (SUNDAYS EXCEPTED), FROM *Pier 28, N. R., foot Murray St.*

4 P. M. in Winter.

THE WORLD RENOWNED STEAMERS

BRISTOL,
Commander A. G. SIMMONS.

PROVIDENCE,
Commander B. M. SIMMONS.

Trains Leave Boston from the Old Colony Depot, corner South and Kneeland Sts., at 4.30 and 5.30 P. M., connecting with the Magnificent Steamers at Fall River.

STEAMERS LEAVE NEWPORT AT 8.30 P. M.

The most direct route to Taunton, Middleboro, Plymouth, New Bedford, Martha's Vineyard, Nantucket, and all points on the South Shore and Cape Cod Railway.

Through Tickets sold to the WHITE MOUNTAINS, and all principal points in New England and the Provinces.

PROMENADE CONCERTS EVERY EVENING
BY
Hall's Celebrated Brass, Reed, and String Bands.

For Tickets and Staterooms

IN NEW YORK—Apply at 241 Broadway, 529 Broadway, Broadway, corner of 23d Street, Dodd's Express Office, 944 Broadway, and 4 Court Street, Brooklyn, or at the Office on the Pier.

IN BOSTON—at No. 3 Old State House, and at Old Colony Railroad Depot.

THROUGH TICKETS sold by all the principal Railroads East, South, and West. Baggage checked to destination.

The only direct Line to and from Newport.

Ask for Tickets via Fall River Line.

J. R. KENDRICK, SUP'T.   A. P. BACON, SUP'T.
O. C. R. R., BOSTON.   N. S. S. CO., NEW YORK.

Saratoga Star Spring Co.

THE SARATOGA STAR SPRING CO. have demonstrated by actual use that the waters from their Spring will keep for Months in their bbls., which are lined with pure tin, and hold its properties as well as in bottles. They now have half bbls. (15 gallons,) being an equivalent of three cases water, which they will lend to customers free of charge, provided they are returned freight paid, and will sell the water at Four Dollars per half bbl. Being less than one-fifth the cost of the same amount of water in pt. bottles, and can be transported for about the price of one case.

Customers can avail themselves of this method of dispensing the water by applying to the Star Spring Co.

PRICE.

Water in half bbls. - - $4 for 16 gals.
Water in qt. bottles, 2 dozen in Case, $5 per Case.
Water in pt. " 4 " " $7 per Case.
Water in bbls. to dealers (equivalent to six Cases) $7.50.

Address

SARATOGA STAR SPRING CO.,
SARATOGA, NEW YORK

MELVIN WRIGHT, Supt. and Gen. Agt.

Citizens' Steamboat Co.

OF

TROY.

THE STEAMERS

Sunnyside and Thos. Powell

WILL LEAVE

NEW YORK, Daily, (Saturdays excpt'd) at 6 o'cl'k, P.M.

From Pier 49, Leroy Street.

RETURNING, WILL LEAVE

TROY, from foot Broadway, Daily, (Saturdays excpt'd)

At 6 o'clock, P. M.

☞ Passengers ticketed and baggage checked via R. & S. and T. & B. Rail Roads to points North and West.

☞ Shippers will mark their freight via "Citizens' Steamboat Co."

G. W. HORTON, Agent, Troy.   JOSEPH CORNELL, Gen'l Sup't, N.Y.

THE
SARATOGA GEYSER, or SPOUTING SPRING.

The Proprietors of the Geyser Spring would respectfully call the attention of Physicians, Druggists, and others to the following analysis of the Geyser Water, made by Professor C. F. Chandler, Ph. D., of Columbia College School of Mines, a few weeks after its discovery:

Chloride of Sodium	562.080 grains.
Chloride of Potassium	24.634 "
Bromide of Sodium	2.212 "
Iodide of Sodium	0.248 "
Fluoride of Calcium	trace
Bicarbonate of Lithia	7.004 "
Bicarbonate of Soda	71.232 "
Bicarbonate of Magnesia	149.343 "
Bicarbonate of Lime	170.392 "
Bicarbonate of Strontia	0.425 "
Bicarbonate of Baryta	2.014 "
Bicarbonate of Iron	0.979 "
Sulphate of Potassa	trace
Phosphate of Soda	trace
Biborate of Soda	trace
Alumina	trace
Silica	0.65 "
Organic matter	trace
Total solid contents	991.546
Carbonic Acid Gas in 1 U. S. Gal.	454.082
Density	1.011
Temperature	46° Fah.

The water never varies in flavor, nor are its properties subjected to change by the dilution of fresh water or the mingling of foreign substances during the wet seasons of the year. As a medicinal agency, its effects are marvelous. Testimonials from all quarters are received, bearing witness to its wonderful cures of diseases.

Geyser Water is put up in Pint and Quart Bottles. Carefully packed for shipment to any part of the globe.

It is boxed in cases containing 4 doz. Pints, 2 doz. Pints, 2 doz. Quarts; it is also sold in metallic lined barrels, upon special application.

Address,

GEYSER SPRING,
Saratoga Springs, N. Y.

New York Central
AND
HUDSON RIVER RAIL ROAD.

Nine Express Trains daily from the

Grand Central Depot, New York,

4th Ave & 42nd St.

TWO SPECIAL DRAWING ROOM TRAINS

FOR

SARATOGA AND LAKE GEORGE,

(From New York to Saratoga in less than 6 hours.)

Five Through Trains from New York to

NIAGARA FALLS.

The best managed Rail Road in the country.
The most complete in all its appointments,

ALWAYS ON TIME.

Wagner's elegantly furnished Drawing Room Cars run on all through trains.
Sleeping Cars of the line unsurpassed.
The best Route from New York to the West.

J. M. TOUCEY, Supt.   **C. H. KENDRICK**, Genl. Ticket Agt.

SARATOGA HIGH ROCK SPRING.

The proprietors of this WORLD-RENOWNED FOUNTAIN have the gratification of announcing to dealers in, and consumers of Mineral Water, that having, at a very great expense, put this spring in the most perfect condition, they are fully prepared to supply all orders for water, either in glass or bulk.

Analysis by Prof. C. F. Chandler, of Columbia College.

Chloride of Sodium,	.	390,127 grs.	Bicarbonate of Magnesia,	54,924 grs.
Chloride of Potassium,	.	8.974 "	Bicarbonate of Soda, . .	34,888 "
Bromide of Sodium,	.	0.731 "	Bicarbonate of Iron, . .	1,478 "
Iodide of Sodium,	.	0.086 "	Phosphate of Lime, . .	trace.
Fluoride of Calcium,	.	trace.	Alumina, ...	1,223 "
Sulphate of Potassa,	.	1,608 grs.	Silica, ...	2,260 "
Bicarbonate of Baryta,	.	trace.		
Bicarbonate of Strontia,		trace	TOTAL, . . .	628,039 grs.
Bicarbonate of Lime,	.	131,739 grs.	Carbonic Acid Gas,	409,458 cub. in.

PRICES—Retail less than 12 dozen.

Quarts, in Boxes of 2 dozen, 3 dozen and 4 dozen, . . . $3 each per doz.
Pints, in Boxes of 4 dozen, 5 dozen and 6 dozen, . . 2 each per doz.

WHOLESALE PRICES PER GROSS.

Quarts, in Boxes of 2 dozen, 3 dozen and 4 dozen, . . $2.50 each per doz.
Pints, in Boxes of 4 dozen, 5 dozen and 6 dozen, ... 1.75 each per doz.

WATER IN BULK.

20c. per gal. to parties furnishing bbls. | 25c. per gal. if bbls. are loaned by Co.
Metal-lined Barrels for sale at cost price, and also loaned to responsible parties. Bottles re-filled at the usual rates.

H. UNDERWOOD, Sup't.   WM. G. FARGO, Pres't.

Address all orders and communications to the Superintendent, at Saratoga Springs.

Adirondack Company's Railroad

FROM SARATOGA SPRINGS

to LUZERNE, HADLEY, THURMAN, (he station for LAKE GEORGE and WARRENSBURG,) THE GLEN, RIVERSIDE and NORTH CREEK,

FORMING THE

MOST DIRECT RAILROAD ROUTE

TO THE

VALLEY OF THE UPPER HUDSON

and the Wilderness.

Connections are made at Thurman with a First-Class Stage Line to Lake George.

The distance by Stage (9 miles), Through Fare, and Time being the same as by the old route via Glen's Falls. This route affords

New and Far More Picturesque and Delightful Scenery

Than any other route from Saratoga.

At Riverside Station, stages connect, running to SCHROON LAKE, CHESTER, POTTERSVILLE, and the NORTH WOODS.

From North Creek, stages run to the "FOURTEENTH," the most desirable rendezvous and starting point from which to reach RAQUETTE LAKE and the HEART OF THE GREAT FOREST.

Express trains leave Saratoga Springs on arrival of Morning and Mid-day trains from the south.

C. E. DURKEE,
General Ticket Agent.

C. H. BALLARD,
Superintendent.

DRS. STRONG'S
REMEDIAL INSTITUTE,
SARATOGA SPRINGS, N. Y.

This institution was established in 1855, for the special treatment of Lung, Female, and various Chronic Diseases, and as a Summer Resort during the visiting season.

The Institute has recently been doubled in size to meet the necessities of its increased patronage. It is now the largest health institution in Saratoga, and is unsurpassed in the variety of its remedial appliances by any in this country. In the elegance and completeness of its appointments it is unequaled. The building is heated by steam, so that in the coldest weather the air of the house is like that of midsummer.

The proprietors, Drs. S. S. and S. E. STRONG, are graduates of the Medical Department of the New York University, and are largely patronized by the medical profession.

In addition to the ordinary remedial agencies used in general practice, they employ the EQUALIZER, OR VACUUM TREATMENT, ELECTRO-THERMAL BATHS, SULPHUR AIR-BATHS, RUSSIAN BATHS, TURKISH BATHS, HYDROPATHY, SWEDISH MOVEMENT CURE, OXYGEN GAS, GYMNASTICS, HEALTH LIFT, MINERAL WATERS, &c., &c.

The fact that a disease is long standing, is generally evidence that it should be treated at an institution having special facilities, for if it could be cured in ordinary practice it should not have become chronic.

REFERENCES:

BISHOP M. SIMPSON. PROF. TAYLOR LEWIS, LL.D.
REV. T. L. CUYLER, D.D. CHAUNCEY N. OLDS, LL.D.
ROBERT CARTER, ESQ.

For particulars of the Institution send for circulars on Lung, Female, and Chronic Diseases, and on our Appliances. Address,

DRS. S. S. & S. E. STRONG,
REMEDIAL INSTITUTE,
SARATOGA SPRINGS, N. Y.

HENRY C. HASKELL,
ALBANY IRON AND MACHINE WORKS,

Nos. 50, 52, 54, and 56 Liberty and 8 Pruyn Sts.

Office, 8 Pruyn Street, near Steamboat Landing,

ALBANY, ... NEW YORK.

MANUFACTURER OF ALL SIZES OF

STEAM ENGINES AND BOILERS,

BRIDGE AND ROOF BOLTS,
CEMETERY, AREA, AND STOOP RAILINGS;

Bank Counter, Office, and Desk Railings;

IRON WORK OF ALL KINDS.

Balconies, Verandas, Iron Bridges,
Bedsteads, Bank Vaults, Wrought-Iron Beams,
Roof Crestings, Doors and Shutters.

MANUFACTURER, ALSO, OF

REZNER, STONE & CO'S

Patent Improved Wrought-Iron Tubular Arch Truss Bridge.

A Lithograph, giving full details, will be sent on application.

CASTINGS OF EVERY DESCRIPTION FURNISHED DAILY.

Particular attention given to Repairing all kinds of Machinery and Boilers.

Patterns and Models made at short notice.

Send for Illustrated Catalogue.

BALLSTON SPA ARTESIAN LITHIA SPRING.

The water of this remarkable Spring is shown by analysis to be twice as rich in valuable Remedial Agents as any other water found in Saratoga County, and to surpass in excellence all the Waters found in other parts of the United States. Flowing from a depth of six hundred and fifty feet, through a tube bored into the solid rock, it is not diluted or contaminated by surface water, as is generally the case with shallow springs.

Its medical properties partake of the most celebrated Springs of the world, and in fact combine the ingredients of all the principal ones in Europe and America. It is very strongly impregnated with *that valuable mineral, Lithia, which is so effectual in dissolving the Chalk, or Limestone and Urate,* deposits in RHEUMATISM, GOUT and GRAVEL, and has been successfully used by hundreds in these diseases, with quick and telling effect; as also in KIDNEY DISEASE, LIVER COMPLAINT, CATARRH, DYSPEPSIA, BILIOUSNESS ACIDITY OF THE STOMACH, CONSTIPATION and PILES, and has proved itself a perfect panacea for these difficulties.

The large quantities of Lithia, Bromine, and Iodine which it contains, specially recommend it to the attention of every Physician.

ANALYSIS BY PROF. C. F. CHANDLER, PH. D.

Chloride of Sodium	750.030 grains.	Sulphate of Potassa	0.520 grains.
Chloride of Potassium	33.276 "	Phosphate of Soda	0.050 "
Bromide of Sodium	3.643 "	Biborate of Soda	trace.
Iodide of Sodium	0.124 "	Alumina	0.077 "
Fluoride of Calcium	trace.	Silica	0.761 "
Bicarbonate of Lithia	7.750 "	Organic Matter	trace.
Bicarbonate of Soda	11.928 "		
Bicarbonate of Magnesia	150.602 "	Total per gall. (231 cubic in.)	1233 246
Bicarbonate of Lime	238.156 "		
Bicarbonate of Strontia	0.867 "	Carbonic Acid Gas	426.114 cub. in.
Bicarbonate of Baryta	3.881 "	Density	1.0159 "
Bicarbonate of Iron	1.581 "	Temperature	52 deg. F.

School of Mines, Columbia College, N. Y., April 21, 1868.

For the benefit of those who are not acquainted with the richness of the different Springs, we give a Statement of the quantity of mineral matter contained in one gallon of Water of the Springs which claim to be the most effective in disease:—

Ballston Artesian		Star Spring	613.683 grains.
Lithia Spring	1233.246 grains.	Seltzer Spring	401.680 "
Congress Spring	567.943 "	Excelsior	514.746 "
Empire Spring	496.352 "	Gettysburgh Katalysine	966.930 "
High Rock Spring	628.038 "		

The Water is carefully and securely bottled, and packed in boxes of four-dozen Pints, and will bear transportation to any part of the world.

To prevent imposition, the corks are marked thus: **Artesian Spring Co., Ballston, N. Y.**

Address,

ARTESIAN LITHIA SPRING CO.,
Ballston Spa., N. Y.

HOWE'S CAVE,

SCHOHARIE COUNTY, N. Y.

Entrance within a few rods of the Station, on the Albany and Susquehanna R. R., 30 miles from Albany.

This is one of the most remarkable curiosities in the United States. For beauty, variety and extent, it is only equaled by the Mammoth Cave of Kentucky, with the advantage of being more convenient of access, and without danger. To increase the novelty, means have recently been taken to have it

LIGHTED WITH GAS

as far as the Lake. Visitors now have the choice of viewing that portion of the Cavern by Torch Light or by Lanterns.

The Only Cave in the World Lighted with Gas.

Full description of the prominent points of interest will be found in this GUIDE, under the Albany and Susquehanna Railroad Division.

For the accommodation of visitors there has recently been erected at the mouth of the Cave a first-class hotel, with all the modern improvements, known as the

CAVE HOUSE.

H. FRANCISCO, Proprietor,

Where every comfort and convenience will be provided to make it pleasant for visitors. Suitable apparel will also be furnished for ladies and gentlemen entering the Cave, although there is less necessity for it now than formerly, as excavations have been made, and are being made, rendering the passage of that portion usually visited easy of access, and extra clothing unnecessary.

Experienced Guides will accompany Visitors either by day or night.

Central Hotel.

W. C. KEYES & SON, Proprietors.

This House is pleasantly located on

MAIN STREET,

Within a very short distance of the Lake, in the beautiful village of

COOPERSTOWN, N. Y.

SUMMER TOURISTS and TRAVELERS,

All the year round, will find all the necessary conveniences and comforts of a

FIRST-CLASS HOTEL.

STABLING ATTACHED.

And Carriages will convey Guests to and from the Railway Station, free of charge.

SMITHSONIAN HOUSE,

The Pleasantest Hotel in the Pleasant Village of

NYACK-ON-THE-HUDSON.

City Comforts, Most Healthful Location, Large, Airy, Well-furnished Rooms, Gas, Pure Water, Shaded Grounds, Magnificent Views, Boating and Riding easily attainable, Good Table.

Transient as well as Permanent Boarders will be made welcome.

PRICES REASONABLE.

ADDRESS

M. L. BIGELOW,

Nyack-on-the-Hudson.

BARDWELL HOUSE,

RUTLAND, VERMONT.

CRAMTON & SALSBURY, Proprietors.

This large and commodious Hotel, is located near the Railway Station and in the business center of the town. It has long enjoyed a reputation as a popular place of resort for travelers, as a first-class house in Vermont. The house has recently been thoroughly renovated, and large and pleasant suites of rooms added; a large Billiard-Room opened; and new furniture and carpets introduced. A wing of fifty feet, three stories high, has been added during the last season, to meet the demands of a continual increase in business.

The house is under the direction of the popular and experienced manager, Major Salsbury, who has been long known to travelers, and will continue in the future, as in the past, to meet the wants and merit the patronage of the public. A first-class LIVERY STABLE is attached to the house, where guests can be at all times accommodated at reasonable rates.

Persons desiring to visit the remarkable

SPRINGS AT MIDDLETOWN,

OR THE CELEBRATED

CLARENDON SPRINGS,

will find Rutland a favorable point to stop.

The Drive to both these places from Rutland is Pleasant and Agreeable.

C. W. BILLINGS,
MARBLEIZED SLATE AND
MARBLE MANTEL WORKS,
Corner North Third and Hutton Sts.,
TROY, N. Y.

MANTELS OF EVERY GRADE,
From the Plain Chamber to the Elegant Parlor and Library Mantel.

MANUFACTURED FROM REAL MARBLE,
OR SLATE MARBLEIZED,

in exact imitation of all the costly imported marble, embracing

EGYPTIAN,	SPANISH,	GALWAY GREEN,
CALIFORNIA,	PORPHYRY,	
SIENNA BROCATEL,		VERD ANTIQUE,
PYRRENESE,		ROMAN,
JASPER,	LISBON,	BLACK and GOLD.

Also executed in imitation of

OAK, WALNUT, ASH AND MAPLE.

ORIGINAL DESIGNS

executed to ARCHITECT'S drawings in any and every style. Grates for hard or soft coal, with summer pieces to correspond with the various styles. Also Black Boards, Sinks, Floor Tiles, Hearths, &c. These Mantels can be securely packed and shipped to any part of the country. Orders for any article capable of being manufactured from slate will be promptly executed. Sufficient inducements will be offered to WHOLESALE DEALERS.

SOMETHING NEW.
THE GOLDEN SUN FIREPLACE HEATER.
WE OFFER TO THE TRADE
The Most Perfect Base-Burning and Illuminating Fireplace Stove
OF THIS AGE.

Our patent arrangement for REMOVING THE SLATE AND CLINKERS FROM THE FIRE-CHAMBER, without dropping the fire out, is an improvement not found in any other Fireplace Heater. This can be done every morning with less trouble than it takes to rake the old kind of Stoves, and a continuous fire be kept going, always fresh on the grate. By this means the entire surface of the stove can always be relied on for heat; but in other stoves, when the grate surface becomes covered with clinkers and the cylinder half filled with ashes and clinkers, only the upper surface will afford heat,—thus very often resulting in the over-heating and ruining of the stove. With our IMPROVED GRATE the base of the stove is always hot. In this stove we give A BOTTOM AS WELL AS A TOP VIEW OF THE FIRE; whereas, in all other stoves the fire can only be seen from the top. With this improvement we can always see through the windows in the base, and tell when the fire requires raking.

In addition to the above-named improvements, we have placed our HOT-AIR DAMPER in the casing of the stove. This improvement saves the trouble of putting a chimney-iron and hot-air damper in the throat of the chimney, as with our improvement the heat can all be thrown down stairs at pleasure. Again, we have made our front circle movable. The stove can be set in and the front put on after the pipe is connected. This gives the workman a chance to see what he is doing while connecting the pipe, and he can always be sure that his pipe is properly connected.

The construction of the Grate and Firepot is entirely new, as well as our Hot-Air Damper,—nothing of the kind having heretofore been invented. The Patent Office at Washington has been thoroughly searched, and no invention bearing any resemblance can be found; consequently we claim "something new under the sun."

We invite the Trade and the Public generally, to call at our warerooms and examine the SUPERIORITY OF THIS STOVE OVER ALL OTHERS.

JAMES SPEAR & CO.,
Inventors, Patentees, and Sole Manufacturers,
1116 and 1118 Market Street, Philadelphia, Pa.
FOR SALE BY
R. L. ROSSMAN, ... Hudson, N. Y.
TROWBRIDGE & SHERRILL, . . . Poughkeepsie, N. Y.

Forest Mining and Slate Co.,

HYDEVILLE,

RUTLAND COUNTY, ... VERMONT.

A. W. HYDE, President.
PITT W. HYDE, Agent.

MANUFACTURERS OF

MARBLEIZED SLATE AND MARBLE MANTELS,

CHIMNEY-PIECES, TABLE-TOPS, PIER-TABLES, CHESS-TABLES, BRACKET-SHELVES, BUREAU-TOPS, AND SLATE BILLIARD-TABLE BEDS, HEARTHS, BLACKBOARDS, FLOOR-TILE, SINKS, WASH-TUBS, BATHING-TUBS, WALKS, GRAVE-COVERS, GRAVE-MARKS,

CHIMNEY-COVERS, ROOFING-SLATE, &c.

ALSO,

Marble Billiard-Table Beds, Tile, Furniture-Tops, &c.

EMPIRE HEATING RANGE

First Premiums at N. Y. State Fairs.

1868, 1869, 1870, 1871 and 1872.

AWARDED FIRST PREMIUMS
AT
NEW YORK STATE FAIRS,
1868, 1869, 1870, 1871 and 1872.

Will Heat from one to four upper rooms in the coldest weather.

MANUFACTURED BY
SWETT, QUIMBY & PERRY,
277 River Street, Troy, N. Y.

FOR SALE BY
R. L. ROSSMAN, Hudson, N. Y.
GEORGE L. DENNIS, Poughkeepsie, N. Y.

PHŒNIX MUTUAL
Life Insurance Company,
HARTFORD, CONN.
January 1st, 1873.

POLICIES ISSUED, 1872, 10,527. **INCOME, 1872, $3,413,752.45.**

The Only old Company of Consideration that has Increased its Business in 1872.

ASSETS, securely invested, - - - - - - - - - $8,299,325.07
SURPLUS, free of all liabilities, - - - - - - - - 1,199,431.50
DIVIDENDS, paid to Policy-holders during the year, - - - - 943,441.71
INCOME, for the year, - - - - - - - - - 3,413,752.45
LOSSES, paid during the year, - - - - - - - - 831,116.32

COMPARISON OF THE BUSINESS OF 1871 AND 1872.

	POLICIES ISSUED.	INCOME.	DIVIDENDS PAID POLICY-HOLDERS.	LOSSES BY DEATH.	NET ASSETS.
1871,	10,039	$3,135,736.14	$663,654.22	$652,500.57	$7,356,967.28
1872,	10,527	3,413,752.45	943,441.71	831,116.32	8,299,325.07

An increase which affords most convincing proof of the growing and well-merited favor with which the Company is regarded by insurers.

The following table exhibits the progress of the Company during the last ten years:

	POLICIES ISSUED.	INCOME.	DIVIDENDS PAID POLICY-HOLDERS.	LOSSES BY DEATH.	ASSETS.
1862 and 63,	1,717	$125,672.00	$1,244.00	$58,000.00	$437,933.00
1864 and 65,	6,590	789,733.00	2,388.00	117,200.00	903,285.00
1866 and 67,	9,919	2,027,651.00	50,222.00	196,050.00	2,218,344.00
1868 and 69,	16,852	4,363,812.00	461,710.00	502,544.00	5,081,975.00
1870 and 71,	19,105	5,963,392.00	1,162,412.00	1,153,056.00	7,510,614.00

An examination of the above figures shows that the Company is a progressive one, that it guarantees ample security to its Policy-holders, and that it affords Insurance at the lowest rates. It appears, also, that within the last ten years it has paid to its Policy-holders, in Dividends, nearly

TWO MILLION SEVEN HUNDRED THOUSAND DOLLARS,
And in losses by death nearly
THREE MILLION DOLLARS,

And at the same time it has greatly increased its Assets, as well as maintained a large surplus over all Liabilities. Since the commencement of its business the Company has issued over

SEVENTY-TWO THOUSAND POLICIES,
And has paid to the families of its deceased members nearly
THREE AND A HALF MILLION DOLLARS.

J. F. BURNS, Sec'y.   **E. FESSENDEN, Pres't.**

Manufacturers of the Celebrated

CALIFORNIA PALE ALE, CREAM AMBER, XX, XXX ALES and PORTER,

Nos. 24, 26 and 28 North Ferry Street, Albany, N. Y.

THE BUCKEYE
MOWER AND SELF-RAKING REAPER.

Styles, Sizes and

PRICES TO SUIT ALL

Classes of Farmers.

The Superiority of the Principles and Mechanism of this Machine have Earned for it its Reputation as the

MOST PERFECT AND
MOST DURABLE HARVESTER
IN THE WORLD.

The high standard of excellence in

MATERIAL AND WORKMANSHIP

maintained, and VALUABLE IMPROVEMENTS ADDED.

MANUFACTURED BY
ADRIANCE, PLATT & CO., 165 Greenwich Street,
NEAR COURTLANDT STREET, NEW YORK.
MANUFACTORY, POUGHKEEPSIE, N. Y.

SKILL LINE STEAMERS,

From Pier 35,

FOOT OF FRANKLIN ST.

old Spring, Cornwall Landing, Rhinebeck, Tivoli, Malden, Smith's Dock and Germantown.

Passage, ONE DOLLAR.

THE PALATIAL STEAMER

NEW CHAMPION,

A. P. BLACK, Commander,

Will leave Franklin St., Mondays, Wednesdays & Fridays,

AT 6 O'CLOCK, P. M.

Making the usual landings.

THE PALACE STEAMER

ANDREW HARDER,

P. H. KNICKERBACKER, Commander,

Will leave Franklin St., Tuesdays, Thursdays & Saturdays,

AT 5 O'CLOCK, P. M.

Making the usual landings.

Arriving at Catskill at 5 A.M., connecting with all lines of Stages.

Returning leave Catskill at 6 P. M. on alternate days.

This Line connects with Steamer City of Hudson for Coxsackie, Stuyvesant, New Baltimore, and Castleton.

SKILL LINE STEAMERS,

From Pier 35,

FOOT OF FRANKLIN ST.

old Spring, Cornwall Landing, Rhinebeck, Tivoli, Malden, Smith's Dock and Germantown.

Passage, ONE DOLLAR.

THE PALATIAL STEAMER

NEW CHAMPION,

A. P. BLACK, Commander,

Will leave Franklin St., Mondays, Wednesdays & Fridays.

AT 6 O'CLOCK, P. M.

Making the usual landings.

THE PALACE STEAMER

ANDREW HARDER,

P. H. KNICKERBACKER, Commander,

Will leave Franklin St., Tuesdays, Thursdays & Saturdays.

AT 5 O'CLOCK, P. M.

Making the usual landings.

Arriving at Catskill at 5 A.M., connecting with all lines of Stages.

Returning leave Catskill at 6 P. M. on alternate days.

This Line connects with Steamer City of Hudson for Coxsackie, Stuyvesant, New Baltimore, and Castleton.

Count the Cost.

THE BEST IS THE CHEAPEST.

It is an undoubted fact that there are but very few families that can afford to do without a Sewing Machine. The question is not "Shall we get one?" but *Which* shall we

GET?"
GET one that **runs easily.**
GET one that **works quietly.**
GET one that **will stay in order.**
GET one that **will do all you need.**
GET one that **has in itself all the necessary parts of a good machine.**
GET one that **adds to all the above** many new and desirable qualities, that can only be had with the

FLORENCE
SEWING - MACHINE.

SEND FOR   Agents Wanted

A FULL   WHERE NOT

DESCRIPTIVE   ALREADY

CIRCULAR.   ESTABLISHED.

FLORENCE SEWING-MACHINE CO.,
FLORENCE, MASS., or

778 Washington Street, Boston.   39 Union Square, New York.

www.ingramcontent.com/pod-product-compliance
Lightning Source LLC
Chambersburg PA
CBHW030248170426
43202CB00009B/663